Lucy Prebble

The Effect

Introduction by Miriam Gillinson

methuen | drama
LONDON • NEW YORK • OXFORD • NEW DELHI • SYDNEY

METHUEN DRAMA
Bloomsbury Publishing Plc
50 Bedford Square, London, WC1B 3DP, UK
1385 Broadway, New York, NY 10018, USA
29 Earlsfort Terrace, Dublin 2, Ireland

BLOOMSBURY, METHUEN DRAMA and the Methuen Drama logo
are trademarks of Bloomsbury Publishing Plc

First published 2012 by Methuen Drama

Published, with changes to the script, in the Methuen Drama Modern Classics
series in 2016
Reprinted 2017 (twice), 2018 (twice), 2019, 2020 (twice), 2023 (twice), 2024

A catalogue record for this book is available from the British Library.

A catalog record for this book is available from the Library of Congress.

ISBN: PB: 978-1-4742-7201-8
ePDF: 978-1-4742-7202-5
ePub: 978-1-4742-7203-2

Series: Modern Classics

Typeset by Fakenham Prepress Solutions, Fakenham, Norfolk NR21 8NN
Printed and bound in Great Britain

To find out more about our authors and books visit www.bloomsbury.com
and sign up for our newsletters.

Introduction

Miriam Gillinson

By the time 'The Effect' premiered at The National Theatre in 2012 Lucy Prebble was already a well-established playwright with multiple awards and a certain 'dazzle factor' attached to her name. Her debut play 'Sugar Syndrome' (2003) picked up a cluster of awards and 'Enron', which Prebble describes as 'the corporate world with jazz hands', had made a considerable splash, first at The Royal Court Theatre and later on the West End. But Prebble felt that something was missing from her writing. Whilst her plays had always been praised for their intellectual flair and theatrical energy, the more emotionally charged side of her writing had not yet taken centre stage. With 'The Effect', though, something changed:

> When I saw people visibly moved [by *The Effect*] that was
> profound for me because I'd never done that before. I'd
> written shows that amused people, perhaps annoyed people
> and sometimes informed people, but I had never moved
> anyone before that play. That was a huge deal for me because
> I thought deep, deep down that perhaps I'd never achieve that.

It's perhaps no surprise, then, that 'The Effect', which marks the moment when Prebble began to fully combine the intellectual and emotional aspects of her writing, is all about the human heart.

***

The first flash of inspiration for 'The Effect' came in 2006 when a drug trial run by the American pharmaceutical company Parexel, and held in Northwick Park Hospital in North London, went horribly wrong. Six male volunteers suffered horrific side effects, including organ failure and lost fingers and toes. The trial was dubbed the 'Elephant Man trial' and splashed all over the papers. Prebble was horrified – but she was also intrigued. This failed drug trial was a play in the making:

> The enclosed nature of the trials was immensely theatrical:
> it was time limited and space limited but not it a way that I

had to impose. Not only that but you are literally engaged in a process whereby you're watching human beings trying to work out what their reactions mean, which is exactly what theatre is. It was never going to be a movie, it had to be a play: you want to see the sweat and skin.

The Parexel drug trial provided the intellectual spark for 'The Effect' but the emotional angle was equally important to Prebble, who was keen to use the trial to explore an 'extremely intense and quite damaging love affair'. Alongside this Prebble had been reading a lot about anti-depressants. This had got Prebble thinking about the overlap between the effect of anti-depressants and the effect of love, both of which raise the levels of dopamine in the body. What was the link between anti-depressants and love and to what extent were both love and depression purely chemical experiences? And where exactly did human emotion fit in with all of this?

And so, through a combination of intellectual and emotional inspirations (alongside countless other ideas rattling around in the subconscious), 'The Effect' was born.

***

The skeleton for 'The Effect' was in place; all it needed now was a body and heart. The play would unfold during a four-week drug trial run by a pharmaceutical company called Rauschen. The drug on trial would be a new anti-depressant, designed to increase dopamine levels and thus make the patient 'happier'. A few key details about the trial set-up would have to be changed to allow Prebble to fully explore her ideas. Firstly, Prebble would need a female volunteer in her play. Women are often excluded from phase-one trials due to fertility risks, but Prebble was going to have to make an exception. She couldn't very well explore the cause and effect of love between a man and a woman without featuring, well, a man and a woman falling in love.

Another modification would be required: unlike the Parexel volunteers, Prebble's trialists would be paid for their time. This monetary aspect was important to Prebble, since it would help her to define her central characters, trialists Connie Hall and Tristan Frey. For psychology student Connie, the trial represents a chance to think more deeply about her area of study. But for long-term drifter and trial-aficionado Tristan, the trial is merely an opportunity to earn some extra dosh for travelling. Thus the intriguing idea is established that whilst one patient – Connie – is highly attuned to the possible side effects of the trial, the other patient – Tristan – couldn't care less. He's just along for the ride.

Finally, Prebble needed to find a way to tie together the themes of love and depression in her play. With this in mind, Prebble introduced two more characters into her delicate four-hander: Dr Lorna James and Dr Toby Sealey, both of whom have private and professional links with depression. Dr James, who is in charge of the trial, has suffered severe bouts of depression throughout her life and is deeply sceptical about 'curing' the condition with drugs. Dr James's boss and ex-boyfriend Dr Sealey (Toby) lies at the other end of the spectrum. A leading figure in the psychopharmacological revolution ('the scientific study of the effects of drugs on human behaviour'), Toby is convinced that the chemical solution to all mental health issues lies just around the corner. The two doctors' impassioned debates about the nature of depression and the best way to treat it are some of the most troubling and compelling scenes in Prebble's play.

***

One final element needs to be taken into account, when considering the way in which Prebble pulled her play together after first reading about that failed Parexel trial: the audience. For in 'The Effect', the audience is just as much on trial as Connie and Tristan.

Over the course of the play, as Connie and Tristan fall in love, the audience's reaction to their relationship is massaged and manipulated. We are drip-fed crucial pieces of information about the trial (such as which volunteer is on the placebo) at critical moments. These twists are designed to radically alter our perspective on Connie and Tristan's relationship and the way we feel about the love between them. The characters' back-histories are revealed gradually and this information, too, is engineered to make us rethink our original assumptions. At every twist and turn we are forced to ask the question: what exactly is it that makes us believe in the love between Connie and Tristan and why does this belief change at critical junctures throughout the play?

In the original National Theatre production, directed by Headlong's Rupert Goold and designed by Miriam Buether, the audience was folded into the play in a very literal sense. The compact Cottesloe stage (now the Dorfman) was expertly reconfigured so as to pull the audience into the action. Spectators were sat on clinically coloured benches, as if perched in a posh medical waiting room. Before the play had even begun the idea was planted that the audience, too, was on trial.

This idea of the audience's involvement is clearly established in Prebble's play text. The play opens with the stage direction: '*The Experiment Begins*'. At the interval, Prebble writes: '*End Experiment Here. Wait Fifteen Minutes. Begin Again*'. And at the play's conclusion: '*End Experiment*'. These stage directions establish the idea that 'The Effect' is a live and variable trial; one with new volunteers (the spectators) and a different set of results every night it is performed. Of course, the extent to which the audience is physically folded into the show is down to each individual director and designer, but – regardless of the production design – the audience remains a crucial component of Prebble's play. Without an audience, 'The Effect' is rendered a fascinating, but controlled and closed experiment. With the audience, Prebble's play becomes an unpredictable and untameable thing – and there's no way one can explore the effects of love without a great dollop of chance, spontaneity and surprise.

***

In her introduction to 'Theatre and Feeling', Anne Bogart discusses the audience's attraction to theatre. It sounds a lot like the process of falling in love:

> We are attracted by the sweep of feeling, of emotion, of adrenaline, surges of dopamine and serotonin, and new neural pathways forged in the brain and extending through the entire body. We crave the feelings engendered in the experience of theatre. (p. xiv, 'Theatre and Feeling')

Each visit to the theatre is, in effect, a mini-love affair in which we temporarily fall for the characters, the ideas and the worlds represented on stage. Those 'surges' of dopamine which Bogart references are created by the connections we forge with the characters on stage but they are also teased and augmented by theatrical special effects. According to the tone of a production, a wash of red light might nudge us towards feelings of love or fear; a nursery rhyme might draw us closer to the characters on stage or send us running in terror. Watching a show, then, is a bit like falling in love to a soundtrack created by an off-stage cupid, craftily tugging at our heartstrings from the wings.

There's a crucial scene near the end of the first half, which brilliantly highlights the way that love – for both the characters and the audience – is both an emotional and chemical sensation, one that is deeply human but also strangely 'other'. Connie and Tristan's love is escalating at a dizzying pace and the two are beginning to succumb to its effects. Tristan, a natural born rule-breaker, has smuggled a mobile phone into the clinic. Phones are prohibited because they might interfere with the equipment but Tristan and Connie have long since chucked the rulebook out the window. That is, after all, a wonderful side effect of falling in love: all the normal rules of behaviour seem to slide away. Holed up in different rooms, Tristan and Connie send each other messages on their phones:

> **Tristan** *and* **Connie** *inhabit bodies racked with expectant, alert physicality, aroused and nervy in separate rooms. They begin texting each other on the phones that Tristan provided. Every glowing vibrating missive is a jolt of dopamine; a high, punctuated by a stressful low awaiting the response. They become faster. It has the quality of shared, separate electroshock therapy or cardiac paddles that shock.* (p. 62)

It's a fiercely packed image, in which the conflicting theories about the nature of love crash wildly against each other. The text messages that Connie and Tristan send each other are no doubt full of deeply personal – or perhaps just deeply horny – words. But the way in which these messages are sent is reflective of the chemical nature of love, with each flashing text message mimicking a jolt of dopamine sent surging around the body. So which element, the chemical or human, is really allowing these two to form a connection and which aspect is the audience responding to?

It's interesting to note that this texting scene arises at a point when Connie and Tristan have broken the rules. Are these two becoming closer because they have moved beyond the bounds of the trial or are the effects of the drug merely taking a stronger grip on our volunteers? And are we, the audience, responding to this relationship because we truly believe in the love on stage, or is our response simply the effect of all those text messages – and resulting flashes of light – firing through our brains? In the same way that Prebble used the image of raptors in 'Enron' to visualize the complex idea of debt-transference, here Prebble alights on a seemingly simple but endlessly rippling image to explore the complex relationship between chemicals and feelings when it comes to love.

This idea is flirted with again when Connie and Tristan sleep with each other for the first time. During rehearsals, this scene became known as the 'Lights up lights down' scene and is made up of a series of snatched moments, which Prebble describes as 'a compilation tape of people's love affairs.' Each little glimpse – 'Where will we live?' or 'Ask me who's in charge' – is followed by the stage direction: *'Darkness. Light.'* Just as with the texting scene, Prebble places us at the heart of a simultaneously chemical and emotional experience. As the lights flash up and down and we fall for Tristan and Connie falling for each other we ask the dazed question: Why?

***

The idea of watching – and believing in – love on-stage is a thrilling and mystifying phenomenon, which is tightly bound up with the idea of chemistry. It is a deeply bizarre theatrical conundrum that a pair of actors, reading exactly the same lines under exactly the same conditions, might provoke hugely contrasting reactions from an audience. What is that mysterious and 'extra' component that creates a gorgeous heat around one pair of actors and a limp coolness around another?

When writing 'The Effect', Prebble was – of course – highly attuned to the impact of 'chemistry' in theatre. According to Prebble, chemistry is borne from some sort of imbalance between two actors: 'I think on-stage chemistry – as with love – is often about someone having something you don't have.' In the original National Theatre production, Connie was played by TV-star Billie Piper and Tristan was played by stage stalwart Jonjo O'Neill. Both actors had something the other required:

> What was great about these two characters and actors is that the statuses were good. Jonjo is a much more experienced stage actor than Billie, but Billie has a star quality – and that's not just because she is 'famous'. She has a warm quality that makes people want to be around her. So when we went into the rehearsal room Billie was actually quite deferential towards Jonjo because he knew exactly what he was doing and that mirrored so beautifully and perfectly the nature of the play.

Of course, chemistry is crucial to all successful theatre but rarely more so than with 'The Effect'; without it, the whole experiment risks grinding to a halt. This profound need for a deep connection between the principal actors has had some intriguing side effects of its own. The 'Effect', says Prebble, is a play that has 'sparked marriages and sired children'. Prebble recalls one particular incident involving a European artistic director, interested in staging the play abroad:

> He came to London and he said, 'Babies get born from this play, right?' So many people who work on 'The Effect' end up falling in love. He then told me that he was thinking of hiring his ex-girlfriend for the role of Dr James. I said: do it. The play needs it. He did just that and, of course, they got back together.

***

The connection between 'chemistry' and love explodes into full life during the asylum scene; an encounter, which Prebble believes, reflects the essence of her play. It is here, outside the confines of the trial, that both Connie and Tristan begin to let their guard down and give in to their emotions. Up until this point, notes Prebble, it has all been a game – especially for Tristan:

> I think before the asylum scene Tristan is playing with Connie. He's not a shag-about but he's a huge flirt and he

feels safe in the environment of the trial and he enjoys it. It's not until this moment that Tristan gets in the water with her.

Even in this new environment, Connie struggles to let go of her psychology training and continues to question the 'authenticity' of feelings cultivated in such surroundings:

Connie It's a chemical reaction, is what I'm saying.
Tristan But I'm still me.
Connie No, yes, you're you, but under with influence of something. (p. 46)

The two circle around the play's central concerns, with Connie falling back on intellectual reasoning and Tristan insisting that she place faith in the body, the moment and instinctive emotion. It isn't until Connie and Tristan stop speaking that their situation is irrevocably transformed. Tristan quits reasoning with Connie and instead begins to dance:

Tristan *performs a tap-dance to the music. It is surprisingly good.* (p. 52)

Written down, it looks like a fleeting moment; but anyone who has seen 'The Effect' (as well as Prebble herself) will tell you that this is the moment when Connie and Tristan fall in love. There's something deeply moving about the economy of this scene. With few resources at his disposal, Tristan fashions a pair of tap shoes by sticking a few drawing pins in his sneakers. And then, on a bare stage and with few special effects (except some tinny music from a mobile phone), Tristan dances for Connie. It's an infectiously romantic moment that taps (!) into something almost supernatural about the nature of love; the way that it might transform a stage, a moment or a person with little more than a few drawing pins and a dazzling smile.

There's an equally heart-punching scene in Nick Payne's play 'Incognito' (2014), which touches on similar themes. The play explores a maze of interlocking relationships, one of which is between Margaret and Patient HM (Henry), a man with chronic memory loss. Payne depicts a number of harrowing meetings between the couple, in which Margaret attempts and fails to connect with her chronically forgetful husband. It seems like a hopeless case and, indeed, Margaret is eventually forced to leave Henry. But 'Incognito' ends on the most spectacular note with a scene that seems to reinforce the idea that there is something about mankind, and the love that mankind experiences, which over-rides the limits of the human brain; that there is something of the 'self' that endures even when the brain is left behind. The final stage direction in Payne's play reads:

> **Henry** *plays the melody taught to him by* **Margaret**. *He plays with confidence and fluidity. It's fucking brilliant.* (p. 105)

It looks like such a little scene but, experienced in the theatre, it feels like everything. It is all the answers to the questions we have barely begun to ask about the brain and consciousness and the way in which love, some innate sense of self – whatever you want to call it – might form a bridge between the two.

***

The asylum scene, then, is the moment that the audience becomes wholly invested in the idea of Tristan and Connie's love for each other. It is no coincidence that Prebble folds the idea of depression into her play shortly after this encounter. For Prebble, love and depression cannot be separated and, if one is to believe in the emotional and relational quality of love, then these same beliefs must also be applied to depression:

> I think it's very wrong to look at love as purely relational and depression as something distinct, isolated, chemical. They are both very similar things but we have a great deal of trouble with that. When someone is what we call 'depressed' we don't want to think it is someone else's fault or in relation to something else, but it can be. If we are going to define love relationally – which I do – I wonder whether it is appropriate to think of depression in the same way.

These conflicting theories about the depression – the idea that it is either an isolated and purely chemical condition or a relational and more emotionally embedded disease – are explored in a series of arguments between Dr James and Toby, both of whom attribute

Connie and Tristan's burgeoning relationship to entirely different causes. Dr James, who suffers from depression and refuses to treat it chemically, is convinced that Connie and Tristan's love is skewing the results of the trial. In short, she believes that the lovers' emotions are over-riding the impact of the anti-depressants. Toby, on the other hand, is adamant that Connie and Tristan's relationship is merely a side effect of the drugs. According to Toby, an expert in psychopharmacology, this so-called 'love' between Connie and Tristan is simply a trick the brain is playing on its hosts:

> **Toby**   The body responds a certain way to what it's being given, they can't sleep, they can't eat, they're in a constant state of neural excitement ever since they met, what's the brain going to conclude?
> **Dr James**   You think it mistakes that for love?
> **Toby**   Not even mistakes it, creates it, after. To make sense of the response. (p.56)

In a pair of powerful and eerily mirrored scenes Toby delivers a scientific lecture whilst lovingly handling a carefully preserved brain; meanwhile, later in on the play, Dr James rips a brain to shreds with her bare hands. Whilst Toby believes the brain can be mapped and chemically controlled, Dr James fears – or perhaps hopes – that part of the brain will always lie beyond the reach of science.

***

The scepticism that Dr James feels concerning the chemical treatment of depression is reflected with choking vividness in Sarah Kane's final work, '4.48 Psychosis' (2000). In Kane's devastating play, the protagonist describes her depression as 'that sickness that breeds in the folds of my mind.' She struggles with her clinicians' cool analysis of her gruelling and deeply emotional condition:

> And I am deadlocked by that smooth psychiatric voice of reason which tells me there is an objective reality in which my mind and my body are one. (p. 7)

Later, Kane's unnamed patient tries to describe the causes of depression to a sympathetic doctor: 'Depression is anger. It's what you did, who was there and who you're blaming.' It sounds an awful lot like Dr James's definition of depression: 'It's about an interaction with the world. It doesn't just appear.' Later still, Dr James implores Toby: 'It's not an 'it', we're talking about me. You want to cut a part of me out and call yourself a hero.' Again, this idea is echoed in Kane's play when she writes: 'Please don't switch off my brain by attempting to straighten me out.'

'4.48 Psychosis' and 'The Effect' both explore the way in which depression warps the connection between the brain and the self and ask the complicated question: what do we do if the brain seems to be working against the natural impulses of the person who hosts that brain? Is this a 'defective' state that should be corrected by chemicals, even if it means permanently altering the person in question? Indeed, is such a correction even possible? There is a devilishly arresting moment in Prebble's first full-length play 'The Sugar Syndrome' (2003), in which a paedophile recollects a doctor's attempt to 'cure' his condition using electro-shock therapy:

Tim   It was a French doctor and you had to sign a bit of paper and then you got hooked up.
Dani   To what?
Tim   Some electro-machine.
Dani   And they just fucking electrocute you?!
Tim   No, that's the death penalty. It's tiny, tiny shocks…
Dani   And did it work?
Tim (*considers*)   It made me want to electrocute kids.
(p. 19, AI S3)

It's a funny and frightening interchange, which gently mocks any attempt to 'cure' the brain of deviant or damaging impulses. This idea is pushed to its limits in a harrowing scene in 'The Effect', as we watch Dr James wrestle – openly and agonizingly – with her inability to control her depression and the dark impulses it provokes within her:

Dr James   I want to be happy. I want to work hard. I want to not shout out swear words on the street. I want to sleep. It [the brain] must know this. It must want that too. If it's me. But. Here I am, where my father held me on a climbing frame and I can see my shoes on the bar. Here, how much I like meringue … Here's my respiration control. Here's my impulse to kill myself. Here is my controlling that impulse. 'You're disgusting. And you're only going to get more disgusting. It's too late. This all gets worse and you can't even cope now … And you're weak and you're a coward and you've ruined people's lives. And you should have done it a long time ago and you never will now'. (p. 89)

The scene culminates with a blazing image: '*She tears the brain to pieces with her hands.*' If there is a stronger expression of the conflict between the brain and the self that depression provokes, I've yet to come across it.

***

As 'The Effect' progresses, the scenes around depression and love are drawn closer together until they finally merge and implode. On one side of the stage, Dr James takes to bed with depression. On the other side, Tristan is hospitalized and Connie sat at his bedside. Having tried to 'game' the trial, Connie has inadvertently caused Tristan to take on over-dose, which has left Tristan with transient global amnesia. The chemical haze of early-love has been swept away and all that remains now is loyalty, affection and kindness. Connie tells Tristan: 'You won't believe this but I swear, I would rather get old and argue with you every day than ever love anyone else' (p.96).

The couple's flirty banter is replaced with banal everyday realities. The two talk about bus fares, shoelaces and schedules on a painful and endless loop. In this respect, the entire span of a relationship – from the heady days of initial attraction to the later days of enduring affection – is played out during 'The Effect', only with the timelines strangely warped. A similar technique is used in Duncan Macmillan's play 'Lungs' (2011), which rattles through the ups and downs of the shared-life of two people in love. Again, time stretches in funny ways in Macmillan's play: a thirty second wait for a pregnancy test result seems to last a lifetime and the desolate days following a miscarriage trickle by in a gloomy blur. In both plays, though, the resting points in life are held in place by love.

Both Macmillan and Prebble explore the way in which love seems to stretch the laws of physics, be that the boundaries of time or the supposed limits of the human brain.

For Prebble, this final scene – in which passion has ebbed away and all that is left is an innate instinct to look out for one another – is the most moving moment in 'The Effect':

> For me it was such a beautiful expression of a whole relationship in a lifetime being squeezed down into a moment. The sense of annoyance and repetition that comes with caring for somebody; the idea of trying to connect with them but failing and ending up talking about bus fares and keys, but that being beautiful and hopeful too. I felt that very deeply.

As the trial shuts down and 'real life' takes over, Prebble's definition of love rises to the surface. It is there in the final scene with Dr James, as we watch her – doubled over with depression – reach for the pills that Toby has provided. Dr James might have decided to treat her depression with drugs but this desire to be cured has, implies Prebble, been inspired by love. This delicate interplay between emotional and chemical influences also underpins the final scene between Tristan and Connie, as the two leave hospital *'and walk out into the real world for the first time.'* This is the moment when Tristan and Connie's love affair truly begins. Love, suggests Prebble, is what happens once the dopamine surges have subsided. Love is what endures once the experiment is over.

***

The Effect

A play for four people, in love and sorrow

The Effect opened at the National Theatre, directed by Rupert Goold, and co-produced with Headlong on 13 November 2012.

Doctors

Anastasia Hille	Dr Lorna James
Tom Goodman-Hill	Dr Toby Sealey

Trialists

Billie Piper	Connie Hall
Jonjo O'Neill	Tristan Frey

Director	Rupert Goold
Designer	Miriam Buether
Lighting Designer	Jon Clark
Composer	Sarah Angliss
Sound Designer	Christopher Shutt
Projection Designer	Jon Driscoll

Author's Note

This published text is an account of the play at our first preview and the text changes in content and order during the preview period. Should you be considering performing it I suggest being in touch with the Knight Hall Agency for the most up-to-date version.

The parts were written with specific actors in mind and when it comes to matters of nationality, physical references or the 'tricks' the volunteers perform for each other, the performers should feel free to mould the text around themselves.

/ Slashes indicate overlapping dialogue.

Dialogue in brackets indicates that the audience doesn't necessarily have to hear the detail but the actor may wish to say it.

Characters

Dr Lorna James, *47 years, 59.5 kg, 169cm*
Dr Toby Sealey, *45 years, 91 kg, 188 cm*
Connie Hall, *26 years, 55kg, 163 cm*
Tristan Frey, *30 years, 80 kg, 173 cm*

Experiment begins

Dr James   Have you ever suffered from depression?

Connie *one arm across herself, leaning back slightly.*

Connie   No. I've felt depressed. But.

Dr James   In what way?

Connie   What I mean is, I've been sad.

Dr James   But not depressed.

Connie   No.

Dr James   There's a difference (?)

Connie   Yeah. I –, it's an illness, isn't it.

Dr James   Mm Hm.

Connie   Well, you tell me. I just mean I haven't got an abnormal amount of chemical – in the brain or anything.

Dr James   And that's depression?

Connie   Yeah. Sorry, I –

Dr James   No, I'm interested.

Connie   Just. I'd never say, oh I'm depressed. Well I would, but just meaning sad. You know cos. That's. I'm not. So.

Dr James   You're just sad?

Connie   When I am. I'm sad.

Dr James   K. And there's no chance you could be pregnant?

Connie   No.

Dr James   What contraception are you using?

Connie   None.

Dr James   Are you in a relationship?

Connie   Yup.

Dr James   Are you sexually active in that relationship?

Connie   I have had sex. Um, I hope to have sex again.

Dr James   But you're not having sex at the moment?

Connie   No, not … Right at the moment (!)

Dr James   And what was the date of your last period?

Connie   I always feel like I should know that. A couple of weeks ago?

Dr James   Are you asking me or telling me?

Connie   I am … pretending to know.

Dr James   K. I need your help, Connie. I see men. A lot of men. This is why. Drug trials are safe but you consent for yourself. You can't consent for someone else. So I need to know for sure you're not pregnant.

Connie   Well give me something to wee on and I'll wee on it.

Dr James   Right. Do you smoke?

Tristan *is sat. He leans forward, one foot dancing.*

Tristan   No.

Dr James   Have you drunk alcohol in the last twenty-four hours?

Tristan   No.

Dr James   Have you taken drugs, medicinal or … otherwise in the last six to eight weeks?

Tristan   (*thinks*) Hmm, pretty su – No (!)

Dr James   Have you had any poppy seeds in the last forty-eight hours?

Tristan   Poppy seeds? … No.

Dr James   So if our test for opiates comes back positive I'll assume that's the heroin? Not a bagel?

Tristan   Fine by me (!)

Dr James   Do you or have you ever suffered from irritable bowel syndrome?

Tristan   No.

Dr James   Cancer of the bowel?

Tristan   No.

Dr James   Cancer of the throat, lungs or skin?

Tristan   No.

Dr James   Arthritis?

Tristan   No.

Dr James   Dementia?

Tristan   No.

Dr James   Type 2 diabetes?

Tristan   No.

Dr James   Type 1 diabetes?

Tristan   No.

Dr James   Have you ever been diagnosed with a mental health problem or been in hospital for a period of more than 24 hours?

Tristan   No.

Dr James   K.

Tristan   Done well there then. Full marks for me.

Dr James   I'm not sure avoiding senile dementia is something you can take full credit for.

Tristan   My body can.

Dr James   So you know and accept you must remain within the facility for the four-week period and hand over all electronic devices during that time?

He hands her a phone.

Tristan   One mobile phone. There's no passcode so don't be looking through the photos!

Dr James   You've done this before, I see?

Tristan   A few times I have.

Dr James   Then you know what happens now.

Tristan   I take it I should go somewhere and ...

Dr James   Can do it here if you like I've seen it all before.

Tristan   Uhh. I will if you like ... (!)

Dr James   No.

Tristan   (No!) I'll take myself off and empty myself out.

Dr James   K.

Tristan   You know, you're an attractive woman, Dr James.

Dr James   Thank you, Tristan.

Connie *and* **Tristan** *both clutch specimens of their urine. Hers is paler.*

Tristan   Would you like me to take that for you?

Connie   Pardon? No. Sorry.

Tristan   That's alright.

Connie   Do you work here?

Tristan   No I was just going that way with – So. I'm the same as you. Here.

Connie   Oh I don't, are you allowed to take other people's – ?

Tristan   Probably not. You've got to sign all that shit. I could do anything to it! I won't (!) You don't have to hide it.

Connie   I'm not particularly.

Tristan   Show me then.

Connie   No.

Tristan   It's warm, that's the thing isn't it? But we're warm. If it was cold we'd be dead.

Connie   You need to drink more water.

Tristan   I do! I will. Don't usually get many girls here.

Connie   You a lot of these then?

Tristan   A bit.

Connie   They're alright, are they?

Tristan   Yeah! Used to be better. Now everyone comes in with laptops and headphones, it's a bit more (*gesture*) ... used to be like a social experiment. The hard thing's living in a small space with a bunch of strangers.

Connie   This is a long one.

Tristan   It is it is. Don't worry though.

Connie   I'm not.

Tristan   You might not even be on it, but you can tell. People say they wouldn't do this, people who'd take a pill off a stranger or do a line at a party, bollocks do they know what *that* is. You from the university?

Connie   Yeah.

Tristan   I think they pay you more, you know.

/ **Connie**   What (!)?

Tristan   Yeah. Trials like this they don't want the immigrants they usually get. They need English, so you can, you know, talking isn't, you know, – no trouble how to, uh ... –

Connie   Articulate?

Tristan   (*smiles*) There you go (!) Fuck. Sure you don't want me to carry that for you. Like a gentleman would.

He reaches out for her specimen.

She scowls. She is holding it by the top, uncomfortable.

Connie   No.

Tristan   Can I touch it.

Connie   No!

Tristan   Don't be precious.

Connie   I'm not!

Tristan   Why you holding it like that then, it was part of you a minute ago ...

Connie   I'm just. Nothing (!)

Tristan   I'm teasing.

Connie   I know. I'm not ashamed of it (!)

Connie *goes over and touches his specimen.*

She lets go.

Tristan   Well, You're gonna have to be my friend now.

Admissions procedure. **Tristan** *and* **Connie** *(all volunteers) are changed into clinic outfits. Their blood pressures are taken, alcohol levels checked, weight, height are monitored*

Dr James *looks to her electronic tablet, the modern equivalent of a clipboard, and begins typing on it. When she does this, her words appear on a screen.*

Text, gradually appearing, reads:

First 25 mg dose of agent RLU37 given at timed intervals as of 13th November 2012, 19:11 (or whatever date and time it is).

Dr James *armed with a timing device to measure the dosing intervals, gives* **Tristan** *a pill that has been emptied into a plastic cup and then a plastic cup of water to wash it down with.*

Dr James   5, 4, 3, 2, 1.

He swallows it. His mouth is checked. **Connie** *is next.* **Dr James** *indicated she should wait. She does.*

Dr James   (Cont'd) 5, 4, 3, 2, 1.

Connie takes hers. Her mouth is checked. It continues, theoretically, with other volunteers.

Medical tests are carried out; temperature, weight, height, pupil dilation, reaction and electrodermal response.

Connie *and* **Tristan** *both eat the same amount of the same food from the same sort of trays. They drink the same amount of water from the same plastic cups.*

(Maybe they both have a cannula fitted to their arms.)

Connie *and* **Tristan** *are put into beds, sitting up, and an ECG monitors their hearts.*

Tristan *has blood drawn. He watches the process.*

Blood is drawn from **Connie** *who looks away from it, slightly squeamish. Her heart rate goes wild.*

Connie *looks away, grimacing.*

It ends. She uncrumples. Both have been provided with a juicebox and a biscuit.

Connie   D'you want my biscuit?

Tristan   Thanks but I can't. If I'm one biscuit up and you're one biscuit down that could throw out all of medical science.

She starts to eat her biscuit.

Dr James   Wait here, please.

Dr James *has been administering the tests. She leaves the room at this point but comes and goes throughout.*

Tristan   Where d'you sleep?

Connie   Oh, down the corridor, they showed me.

Tristan   I'm with ten sweaty blokes. You're biologically blessed.

She is biting her nails.

Tristan - (Cont'd) You bite your nails?

She nods, guilty.

He holds his hand out to her to show he does too, badly.

Tristan Me too.

She takes it, looks, smiles.

Connie (*warm*) God (!) They're really bad!

Tristan *sees her wristband.*

Tristan No shit!

Connie What?

Tristan We have the same birthday.

Connie The 29th?

Tristan Yeah!

She looks at his DOB on his band.

Connie Oh yeah!

Tristan How weird is that? The exact same – birthday (!)

Dr James Could you lie down please.

Tristan What are the chances of that!

Connie Actually, I don't think it's that unusual, I mean it's not as unlikely as you'd think.

Tristan How d'you know what I think?

Connie Sorry, than most people would think. I mean in a group of people, the group doesn't actually have to be that big for you to maybe share a birthday. Cos probability-wise you're not saying how likely is it this person was born on a particular date – one in 365 obviously. You're just saying, of *all* the dates, how likely is it that two people in a group have the same?

Tristan Oh. Well I think it's a sign.

Connie   Right.

Tristan   I think we're twins. Identical twins. They decided to raise us in very different environments to see what effect it had long term. Me a quaint little shithole on the coast near Coleraine. And you?

Connie   Basingstoke.

Tristan   Basingstoke. Turned out it had a massive effect.

Dr James   Can you sit down please?

Connie   What are you doing for your birthday?

Tristan   Leaving and never coming back. This is for spending money. I'm going travelling.

Connie   Oh cool!

Tristan   Does your man not mind you doing this then?

Connie   My man? No. I – No, I do what I … like (!)

Tristan   Course you do, it's like that. I got a man but I don't need a man. Beyonce and shit.

Connie   He's away so –

Tristan   Away for work, is he?

Connie   No.

Tristan   Stag do?

Connie   No.

Tristan   Is he in prison?

Connie   What? No! He's visiting family.

Tristan   Oh right. Not with you though.

Connie   No, with a friend.

Tristan   Oh.

Connie   With his son. He's got a little boy. From before.

Tristan   Nice. So you're happy?

Connie   Don't do that.

Tristan   What?

Connie   That. Are you happy thing. That thing guys say when /
they're –

Tristan   / I'm sure you are – !

Connie   Cos who ever actually says, yeah I'm perfectly
completely –

Tristan   Some people do.

Connie   Okay, yeah, well.

Tristan   What?

Connie   I am.

Tristan   What?

Connie   (*unhappily*) Happy!

Tristan   Where would you go? India I'm thinking.

Connie   I don't know. I wouldn't go anywhere exotic actually.
Somewhere American. Not the cities, I mean. The real, the dust,
those states. Somewhere it's horizon on both sides.

Tristan   The plains.

Connie   I'd like to see a wild horse.

Tristan   Aye?

Connie   And hold a gun.

Tristan   Right.

Connie   I wouldn't shoot the horse (!)

Tristan   Why don't you go then?

Connie   Why don't I *go*?

Tristan   Yeah.

Connie   Money, time, life. There's just so much to do.

Tristan   Yeah. It's great.

She laughs, looks at him, intrigued.

We hear their ECGs gradually slow and settle into a calmer rhythm and eventually they beep/beat together.

'DEATH'

The word appears on a screen in a blue font.

Connie and **Tristan**   Blue.

Dr James *types and text reads:*

The Stroop Test.

Volunteers view trigger words but name only the colour in which the word appears. Subject takes longer to distinguish the colour of words that are psychologically relevant or troubling to them.

Various words have appeared on the screen in colour. **Tristan** *and* **Connie***: (separately in theory) have been naming the colours they appear in.*

During above, as needed. (BEAUTY. CHAIR. TEST.)

GUILTY

Connie *names the colour after* **Tristan***.*

BABY

Together.

FATHER

Tristan after.

JOY

Together.

DIET

Connie after.

LONELY

Together.

BREASTS

Tristan after. He's amused.

MEMORY

Together.

BLUE (but in another colour)

Connie   Blue. Shit. Sorry.

She corrects herself. Tristan gets it right.

Dr James   That's okay. It's not that kind of test.

Connie   Dr James.

*It is now just **Connie** and **Dr James**.*

Dr James   Yes.

Connie   Sorry, I don't know if it matters. But I thought I should say. I know about the Stroop Effect. I know it's about how long you take to say the colour, that the more meaningful the word, the longer it takes. I don't know if it matters. If you know.

Dr James   No.

Connie   Really? I thought knowing might make me try to *beat it*.

Dr James   In most cases being aware of your own bias doesn't actually mean you can affect that bias.

Connie   Really?

Dr James   Yes. It's one of life's tragedies. Do you want to hear this story again? You can hear it a total of two times.

Connie   Okay.

Dr James   You open up a dry cleaners. On the border between two towns. Your shop is the only one of its kind in the surrounding area. Your business prospers and reactions from your customers indicate the cleaning is of good quality.

Connie   Okay.

Dr James   You hire more staff which is an outlay but improves customer service, and you wonder about applying to the bank for a loan to open up a chain of such shops. As you had expected the bank approves the loan.

Connie   Go me!

Dr James   Now a quick memory test, can you tell me the nature of your business? Was it A) greengrocers or B) dry cleaners?

Connie   B.

Dr James   And where was the shop set up was it A –

Connie   On the border / between two towns.

Dr James   / In the centre of town or B on the border between – yes. And the reason for your business success, was it A) lack of competition or B) A good business plan?

Connie   (*thinks*) Sorry, what?

Dr James   The reason for your success –

Connie   You didn't say. Is this a test of *memory?*

Dr James   This is the last question.

Connie   A lack of competition or my good business plan?

Dr James   That's right.

Connie   But the business and the town are fictional. Even the me is kind of fictional.

Dr James   Could I have an answer?

Connie   Afterwards will you tell me why?

Dr James   Why?

Connie   I'm a psychology student.

Dr James   Then you can work it out for yourself. What was the reason for your success?

Connie   (*shrugs*) A) Lack of competition. May as well. There'll be like a hundred factors in this fictional town's economy.

Dr James   Okay.

Connie   So if I'd said my business plan.

Dr James   Then what?

Connie   Then I'd be taking responsibility for the success –

Dr James   Right ...

Connie   So what's that got to do with the trial?

Dr James   People prone to depression, Connie, they tend to attribute success to external causes and failure to internal ones.

Connie   So if I do well it's because of something outside of me, but if I do badly it's because of my stupid self.

Dr James   Exactly.

Connie   What would a 'normal' mind do?

Dr James   Well a so-called 'healthy' mind, the healthiest mind would think if things go well it's down to me, I did that. And if it goes badly –

Connie   They've been unlucky.

Dr James   Victim of circumstance, yes. So you're studying psychology?

Connie   (*nod*) And social science.

Dr James   Gosh. Never too late to become a real doctor, you know (!) So is that why you're here, interested in trials?

Connie   Yes, and depression.

Dr James   Mother or father?

Beat.

Dr James   (Cont'd) Sorry. My background's in psychotherapy. How do you feel?

Connie   A bit awkward.

Dr James   I mean physically.

Connie   Oh. Fine. A bit tense you know 'up' like, something's going to happen. I keep thinking my hearing's really good, that's crazy isn't it?! But Tristan said the same.

Dr James   Well the agent's designed to increase levels of dopamine –

Connie   Right.

Dr James   And that's what's stimulated by new, exciting experiences generally so … There's an old joke actually. How does it go. So. There's this medic at a conference and he's fallen for a girl there who hasn't looked twice at him. Now he knows dopamine is the initial trigger in falling in love but also that dopamine is stimulated by new, exciting experiences. So to try and get the girl he arranges for them to go *bungee jumping* together to sort of set up his own chemical reaction. So the instructor ties them together and they stand over this incredible valley and he's got his arms round her and they fall headlong into this incredible, adrenaline filled rush – and their dopamine levels go wild. And eventually, they get lifted back onto the bridge, they get their breath back and he looks into her eyes and says, 'Wasn't that amazing?!' And breathlessly she answers, 'Yes! And isn't the instructor handsome!'

Beat.

Dr James   (Cont'd) It's sort of a science joke so ...

Connie   No, I like it. Cos it's the instructor ...

Dr James   Yes, that she's … yes.

Toby *enters, perusing medical records* **Dr James** *has given him.*

Toby   This is very good isn't it.

Dr James   I'm not sure it's good or bad it's just the case.

Toby   Well done. Different from what you're used to I bet.

Dr James   Different.

Toby   Easier.

Dr James   Different.

Toby   Elevated mood.

Dr James   Yes.

Toby   Increased energy levels.

Dr James   Yes.

Toby   Weight loss (!)

Dr James   Mm-hm.

Toby   And increased height?!

Dr James   Average 2 cm.

Toby   Height?

She nods.

Toby   (Cont'd) Doesn't seem likely.

Dr James   Well I'm not raising the floors.

Toby   I didn't think we were even monitoring height.

Dr James   I monitor everything.

Toby   I see that. Why are you doing psychological tests? Of this quantity. It's a phase 1, physical.

Dr James   Well everything's physical in the end isn't it.

Toby   ... Ok! An anti-depressant effect in healthy volunteers. That'd be extraordinary.

Dr James   Barely a week in, they know they're being given an anti-depressant, it'll be mostly their own expectation, surely?

Toby   Could be. But the new design is fast acting so ...

Dr James   Sorry, I just assume it's psychological.

Toby   Robust objectivity. Quite right. It's good to see you Lorn. I mean I know I saw you at the – but I mean alone. You look really well.

Dr James   –

Toby   I bet you think I'm looking old.

Dr James   What? No, don't say that, you make me think you're thinking that about me.

Toby   No!

Dr James   I should say thank you for all this. I know I wouldn't – it's very um, good of you.

Toby   Oh don't (even) – it's just great to see you and for you to be here. Let's just make sure this is done really well.

Dr James   What does that mean?

Toby   With lack of bias and precision.

Dr James   Well I wasn't just going to circle random numbers, Tobe (!)

Toby   No no no, I'm honestly trying to help. You know how things are. We could do with fresh eyes. It's a touchy area.

Dr James   Rightly so.

Toby   Believe me *I* don't want to spend five weeks on a trial that gets discredited. Why we're developing new gens in the first place.

Dr James   Because the old ones have been discredited.

Toby   They haven't been discredited, the studies that discredited our original trials have themselves been discredited now.

Dr James   In new studies by you.

Toby   Yes. Well us. Don't worry, I'm the one always persuading them not to relocate the trials out to West Africa. Anti-depressant trials!

Dr James   I'm sure they get depressed in Gambia.

Toby   I'm sure they get fucking depressed in the Gambia, doesn't mean we should use them as guinea pigs then disappear off with our drugs.

Mini-beat.

Dr James   I read you were advising the government on psychopharmaceuticals at the moment?

Toby   No, I'm on a panel. I'm not –

Dr James   I keep expecting to see you on a TED talk or something.

Toby   Ah! No I. They have asked actually, but no I'm saving that for the day I write that book (!)

Dr James   And how are you? How are the kids?

Toby   Great, thank you, yeah. I got engaged!

Dr James   Oh! Congratulations! Wow (!)

Toby   Yes and divorced obviously, I should probably say those the other way round.

Dr James   Ah, okay. Well, congratulations again.

Toby   I realize that should probably have happened a while ago …

Dr James   Well. That must have been hard.

Toby   No. For the best. It's all good.

Dr James   No, I think I heard actually, is she a lab assistant at MB?

Toby   Yes, where did you hear that?

Dr James   I ran into Bill Fitzgrove at customs ages ago and he said –

Toby   God Bill, did you, yes, he worked with her –

Dr James   Yeah.

Toby   How is he? Is he still at Brown?

Dr James   Yes. He's Alzheimer's now.

Toby   Great! You mean he's –

Dr James   Oh yeah, researching, he's not … (!)

Toby   Good (!) huh. Yeah. Did we – Did I meet him with you?

Dr James   Yes at that conference.

Toby   My god, yes, and he came over at the bar –

Dr James   That's right. It was after your talk and you / dropped –

Toby   / That's right. I still do that talk –

Dr James   I know.

Toby   Well a variation of it, for Raushen.

Dr James   With the uh?

She mimes an action, carrying a bucket. He mimes it back.

Toby   Yes.

Dr James   (*remembering*) Yes, I remember. He came over after and you dropped your cigarette, and I was hopping about cos it burnt my leg –

Toby   What?

Dr James   You remember. He was introducing himself –

Toby   No, I do, but you dropped it, and – I don't smoke.

Dr James   Of course you don't, nobody smokes *now*, you did then.

Toby   Did I? No I didn't – very ...

Dr James   I have a scar!

Toby   Well to be fair we can't know what caused that (!)

Dr James   No.

Toby   But I'm sorry if that's true.

Dr James   I wasn't being serious. When you could smoke indoors (!)

Beat.

Toby   Really glad to see you looking so well, though, Lorna. /

Dr James   / And you.

Toby   I've got to do one of these trial development seminars tonight, but I'll be back for the scans. I'll sign off first dosage escalation now if you're happy?

Slowly and slightly **Dr James** *nods.*

DOSAGE INCREASE: 50mg

Dosages are administered. (5, 4, 3, 2, 1)

Connie   I've been having the most extraordinary dreams.

Tristan   Yes! Me too.

Connie   Vivid.

Tristan   Yeah! And so fucking ...

Connie   Mundane!

Tristan   Bizarre!

Tristan   (Cont'd) Mundane?

Connie   Yeah, last night I dreamt my whole weekly shop I do. Round the whole supermarket, near where I live. My brain must have designed every label, every detail. In real time, for hours. And when I woke up I was like, what a boring dream! And then I thought, god no, what a boring *life!*

Tristan   One week in, this is where it hits you.

Connie   Yeah I'm feeling that.

Tristan   I'm climbing the fucking walls.

Connie   I'd kill for a cigarette.

Tristan   I snuck out once for a fag.

Connie   Did you?!

Tristan   You know round the back of here's an old asylum?

Connie   What?!

Tristan   You know, a mental hospital.

Connie   No (!) What's it like?

Tristan   You want to see?

Connie   We're not allowed out.

Tristan   I might know a way.

Connie   You mean the really old building with the red brick?

Tristan   Yeah, they don't use it anymore, it's all boarded up.

A man enters with a bucket. It is **Toby***.*

Toby   (*to audience, at an industry event*) Hello. This couldn't be more glamorous, could it, a man coming on with a bucket? But fear not, the money's gone on what's inside. Welcome to Raushen. Don't worry, I'm not going to ask anyone to volunteer but I would love to talk to you about why it's so important that people do. I'm Toby, I'm a psychiatrist, I'm afraid. My father was a heart surgeon and when I told him I wanted to specialize in psychiatry he said, 'Oh *really?* The *Cinderella* of medicine?' Which um, (*he gestures to a knife in his heart, casually*) because dad thought psychiatry was all nonsense about Freud and how we're all obsessed with our parents. So I devoted my life to proving him wrong (!) But seriously, I do think I've vanquished my father in a way because, I didn't want to be a heart surgeon. I didn't want to be a *plumber* of the body. I wanted to be an explorer.

He removes something from liquid in the container and holds it aloft and looks at it. It is a human brain.

Toby   (Cont'd) So I became a psychiatrist and of course, like all doctors, my chosen speciality is defined by what goes *wrong*. When the brain goes wrong, there are symptoms and causes, as with anything else. But because we *think* with our brain we struggle to frame it as a piece of biological machinery. We're happy to have heart transplants and liver transplants but we can't imagine a brain transplant. Because nowadays we think our soul is in here. But that sense of 'us' is only a tiny part of what's going on at any moment. As you sit listening to me your brain is taking care of a lot of things so you don't have to, consciously – your temperature, forcing food through your gut, positioning your spinal column in your seat, which doesn't look terribly comfortable, I'm sorry about that. Swallowing so you don't choke on your saliva. Now if we suffered a neurological oddity that meant we couldn't swallow we'd see nothing wrong with addressing and repairing that in the brain. It's the same with mental health issues. There are diseases of the brain. That doesn't make people crazy or incapable or dangerous in soul. They're ill. We are many of us going to experience a mental health condition in our lifetime. We're past the the notion of the sane and the insane! Why not call ourselves the insane and the 'not insane at the moment'? Managing our mental hygiene is a life's work and part of that is how we medicate or supplement. The psycho-pharmacological revolution is the defining occurrence in medicine in my lifetime. I'm *proud* to have been a part of that. My father lived just long enough to see it. He ran three miles a day into his seventies, he didn't touch red meat, what got him in the end was up here. But in one of his more lucid moments, he decided to donate his brain to science for teaching and research into this field. (*He talks to the brain*) So thank you dad. Thanks to people like you, the Cinderella of medicine got to go to the ball.

Moonlight.

Connie *and* **Tristan** *enter a very large room. It is an unused dilapidated recreation area, once something grander.*

Connie   Oh my word.

She instinctively gets closer to him.

Tristan   Fuuuck.

They laugh. They make noises that echo.

Tristan   Why do they keep it? It's falling to bits.

Connie   It'll be a listed building. It'd probably cost more to do it up than to close off like this.

Tristan   You're such a grown up.

Connie   It's amazing to be somewhere with space.

She enjoys the space. She does something gymnastic.

They share a cigarette.

Tristan   Imagine them all in here, rocking.

Connie   (*re. her gymnastics*) Can you do any tricks?

Tristan   I'll show you on one condition.

Connie   What?

Tristan   Come travelling with me after this.

Connie   (*sound*) !

Tristan   Why not? Doesn't have to be for long. We'll go anywhere you like.

Connie   I'm not going travelling with you. I barely know you.

Tristan   What do you want to know?

Connie   Tris, I'm not doing that, my course, my relationship, my work.

Tristan   Don't be so practical!

Connie   You're the one being practical! For me it's insane!

Tristan   Do you think your parents would like me?

Connie   !

Tristan   Do they like him?

Connie   Piss off.

Tristan   I bet they don't. He must be older, right? Is he older?

Connie   He's in his forties.

Tristan   Oh, nice and vague. Just tell me he's not your teacher or something.

Connie   He's not – stop it.

Tristan   Just tell me it's not that.

Connie   It's not. He never taught *me*.

Tristan   Oh fuck.

Connie   The reason I'm not at all bothered about what you think is I know what you think and I know it's not true.

Tristan   Boring anyway. Let's get back to what do you want to know about me?

Connie   Nothing, Tris, seriously.

Tristan   Nothing?!

Connie   No I do, course I do. You're very interesting. I just feel weird. I don't feel what I'd feel like in real life.

Tristan   This *is* real life. When is it real?

Connie   No I mean. The anti-depressant, the doctor said, they're designed to stimulate certain, like dopamine. Which is the rush you get if something exciting happens or, when you – well it's fake, it's a chemical that feels like. Like falling for someone.

Beat.

Tristan   So?

Connie   So forgive me if I take everything with a big pinch of, you know ...

Tristan   What you think I don't like you properly because of the –?

Connie   I think it's a strong possibility.

Tristan   Bullshit. I can tell the difference between who I am and a side effect.

Connie   With respect Tristan, no you definitely can't.

Tristan   You're saying any attraction is a result of the trial.

Connie   Part of it could be.

Tristan   (*quietly pleased*) You must be basing that on feeling a sort of attraction then?

Connie   I didn't say that ...! It's a chemical reaction, is what I'm saying

Tristan   But I'm still me.

Connie   No, yes, you're you, but under the influence of something. If you were really pissed and going 'I love you, you're my best mate' I wouldn't believe it either.

Tristan   Why not? Men mean it when they say that, they just can't say it when they're sober.

Connie   Yeah but they'll have known that person (ages) – and I don't know, I'm just telling you what the doctor said.

Tristan   Ah, what does she know? They don't know anything, Knowledge is a myth.

Connie   (*unimpressed*) Okay ...

Tristan   They wouldn't be trialling if they knew. One time I had chronic diarrhoea for six days straight, nobody predicted *that*. They say all sorts of shit, they say you have to give in your phone because it *interferes with the equipment*.

Connie   You *do* have to give in your phone because it interferes with the equipment.

Tristan   Jesus, do you want a phone? I'll give you a phone. I gave in a dummy.

He roots around in his bag and tosses her a phone.

Tristan   (Cont'd) Say you have to make a call, get your phone, go to the loo, swap sims. 'Interferes with the equipment', it's like they say that on planes. It's just it's really hard to control a bunch of people if they've all got phones. Anytime anyone says turn off your phone you should worry that's a situation where you might die, not worry about the fucking equipment.

Connie   Can I actually have this?

Tristan   Yeah I normally sell them but that's a shit one.

Connie   I like it, it's like the 90s.

Tristan   You don't really think that? That I only like you, cos I'm high or something.

Connie   Why not? Everything we do is just about what's pumping round us, isn't it?

Tristan   Well that's a cold way of looking at a person.

Connie   Why?! We *are* our bodies, our bodies are us, ... there's not something *more* ... And that's fine. That's enough. It's like, the world is incredible and beautiful, even though we know there's no god behind it. It's even *more* amazing for that.

Tristan   Hang on, we *know* there's no God behind it?

Connie   Yeah, I mean, Sorry. Oh, Really?

Tristan   What?

Connie   You believe in God?

Tristan   What? It's alright, you look disappointed (!)

Connie   No, it's terrible isn't it, you just assume – when you meet someone and you ...

Tristan   When you meet someone ...

Connie   And you get on, you assume ...

Tristan   I knew it! You're disappointed I believe in God because you like me! (Thank you Lord).

Connie   Sorry that's awful.

Tristan   No no no. Let's say you're right, let's say we're attracted to each other, (because we are you just admitted it and you can't take it back) let's say we're attracted to each other and that's been kicked off by these ...

Connie   The dopamine.

Tristan   Drugs or whatever. So what?

Connie   What d'you mean?

Tristan   What difference does it make?

Connie   Well clearly then it's something to be wary of.

Tristan   It is what it is. Doesn't matter why.

Connie   It matters massi – ... It's all that matters.

Tristan   Why?

Connie   Because, It's the *reason!*

Tristan   So?

Connie   I can't work out if I understand something you don't or you understand something I don't.

Tristan   People meet each other and fall in love all sorts of ways, doesn't matter what starts it. I'm sure there's a rush of something chemical if you meet on holiday or on a bus with a bomb on it, doesn't mean Keanu Reeves and Sandra Bullock aren't really in love.

Connie   Are you talking about the movie 'Speed?'

Tristan   Yeah, it was on in the rec room last night. But you think it's fake? So what you think a few years on, Sandra and Keanu are just sat in a restaurant in silence thinking why did I marry this loser, all we had in common was a bus!

Connie   (*laughing*)Yeah I do actually, I do!

Tristan   I like your laugh.

Connie   D'you know why?

Tristan   It's sexy.

Connie   No actually why. It's a show of submission.

Tristan   What?!

Connie   Laughing is a way of showing submission, so men like it when women laugh. It shows they're dominant.

Tristan   In my fuck! You laugh when something's funny.

Connie   No. You don't laugh out loud alone watching a sitcom.

Tristan   Yes you do.

Connie   You don't. It's a social thing … It says 'I get the joke, I'm clever', or you use it to show you're attracted to someone. The head thrown back, the throat exposed.

Tristan   That's not why you laugh. You laugh at something. I've taken drugs before, right? There's not a drug in the world can really make you look at someone find them attractive or listen to 'em and find them interesting or –

Connie   Yes there is!

Tristan   Not smell them and … know.

He's advanced closer and closer until now they can just about smell the other.

Connie   That's pheromones isn't it?

Tristan   Is there no mystery for you?

Connie   There is, but it's more than smelling isn't it. It takes work.

Tristan   That is SUCH a lie. You don't believe that.

Beat.

Connie (*defences down*) I just think it comes and goes. There's a period of time, maybe enough to raise a child and then … . You know, the few times I've ever loved anyone they've always, at some point they've written I Love You in the snow or the sand – on holiday – to me. And it's wonderful, but the next time someone … it happens, or the next even … you think. Oh Okay. Again. And you think of the last time. And what that meant. And, just for it to get washed away or melt or … .

Tristan Some people never get loved like that.

Connie I know.

Tristan If I did that, for you, I'd be holding back the sea from ever coming in.

Connie (*touched*) You're sunshine, you know that. I bet you thought the dry cleaning business was a success cos of your great business plan, didn't you?

Tristan Of course. It was!

Connie So you take drugs then, proper ones?

Tristan / Sometimes. You?

Connie No. I just think of drugs as like fags or cheese or something, if you get to a point and you're not into them, don't get into them you'll only have to give them up down the line cos they're bad for you.

Tristan It's about trying something new.

Connie Sure but it's only new once. Then it's the same as everything else.

Tristan But everything has to be new once!

Connie Sure but it's essentially a way of distracting yourself.

Tristan From what?

Connie From the fact that you and everyone you love is definitely gonna die.

Mini-beat.

Tristan   Good! I'm glad I'm distracting myself from that! Good!

Connie   That thing of oh this thing will make me happy, no this thing, no it must be that next thing. Like why are you going travelling?

Tristan   To see things, meet people. Have my mind … expanded.

Connie   Cool man.

Tristan   What's wrong with that?!

Connie   Nothing.

Connie   Just. Like look at this square metre. (*She's talking about the floor*)

Tristan   What?

Connie   There's a whole world here. It's just what you notice. Look at the floor.

Tristan   Tiles.

Connie   Yeah, used to be. Different colours.

Tristan   Tiny tiles.

Connie   Mosaic. That seems weird.

Tristan   Why would people put a mosaic on the floor of a mental asylum?

Connie   Maybe it wasn't a mental asylum when it was built.

Tristan   Or maybe they thought mental patients spend a lot of time looking down.

She smiles at him.

Connie   See all of this, you can get all of this from one square yard. You don't need to change continent every day.

Tristan   That would work, that would work except for one thing.

Connie   What?

Tristan   You wouldn't have seen any of this if it wasn't for me.

Beat.

Tristan   (Cont'd) Come travelling with me.

Connie   Oh come on – I don't know you, I can't trust you –

Tristan   You've come into a mental asylum with me at night! You trust me. I'm going to see a lunar rainbow. In Zambia, three days a year, the full moon hits this waterfall and it refracts the moonlight. You got that in your square yard?

Connie   Do your trick.

Beat.

Tristan   I could actually.

Connie   I really want to see it.

Tristan   Do you?

Connie   Yeah.

Tristan   (I might go outside your square yard is that okay/)

Connie   (/That's fine)

He cycles through tracks on his phone. He plays one.

He gets drawing pins from an old notice board and stabs them into his soles.

Tristan *performs a tap-dance to the music. It is surprisingly good.*

Tristan   Regional junior Ulster tap champion 1994!

Towards the end he puts his arms around **Connie** *to half-dance with her and leading to a kiss. During,* **Dr James** *enters*

Dr James   Oh thank god, where have you been?! I was about to call the police!

Connie   Sorry.

Dr James   Are you okay?

Connie   Fine.

Dr James   What's going on?

Connie   Nothing sorry.

Dr James   Did you climb out of a window?!

Tristan   No, fire / escape.

Connie   / Fire escape. Sorry.

Dr James   Was there a fire?

Beat as they work out whether this is rhetorical.

Tristan   We were going a bit mad in there and wanted to check out / outside –

Dr James   / Sorry I didn't realize I was in charge of a bunch of school kids –

Connie   Sorry.

Tristan   Sorry.

Dr James   You signed a protocol.

Tristan   We haven't done anything to mess / with the –

Dr James   / You have no idea what you've done. Have you been smoking?

Dr James   (Cont'd) It stinks of it.

Tristan   Alright, but yeah we're not at school, so you don't need to be a bitch/ about it

Connie   / Tris –

Dr James   (*furious*) / Nicotine will inflate your dopamine levels for hours which are already elevated from the agent, that affects my results. I'm sorry if my experiment that you're being paid to do is getting in the way of your moves.

Dr James   (Cont'd) Connie?

Connie   Mm?

Dr James   You came here willingly, I assume?

Connie   Yes!

Tristan   Steady (!)

Dr James   Just to be clear, you have signed a consent form committing to refraining from sexual activity.

Connie   Yeah, I know (!) Not that we've done anything … (!) Other than what you saw.

Tristan   Yeah, you perv.

They both look at him.

Tristan   (Cont'd) Sorry I don't know why I said that.

Dr James   You can't disappear with psychiatric medication coursing through you, I'm responsible for your safety –

Connie   Sorry.

Dr James   Bed please. We have fMRIs tomorrow, go and rest your brains.

Dr James *lights a cigarette and smokes it and hears herself over the speaker. As she hears her own voice she tries to control a swelling sobbing growing in her from anxiety.*

Dr James   (v/o) Okay. Just relax. Everything's fine. Exhale. There's no need for anxiety. Just keep your head in one place. Okay. Now I want you to think of something positive. They think of one another.

Connie   Tristan.

Tristan   Connie.

During above, their beds become MRI machines and the loud, otherworldly, claustrophobic darkness of MRI envelopes each lover in their own minds.

Scans of two brains, theirs, on screen.

Importantly, which scan belongs to which volunteer is unknown.

Observing the two brains cans are **Toby** *and* **Dr James**.

Toby   What do you think?

Dr James   What do *I* think?

Toby   Yeah, what do you think?

Dr James   I think it's too early to say.

Toby   What?!

Dr James   I think it's too early to say.

Toby   Dampened amygdala activity.

She nods.

Toby   (Cont'd) Strong activity in the dopaminergic pathways and the reward centres of the brain in general. An anti-depressant effect if ever I've seen one!

Dr James   If you say so.

Toby   (Cont'd) It's on a scan, Lorna, right in front of you!

Dr James   I don't doubt there's an 'anti-depressant effect' going on. But I don't think it's got anything to do with your drug.

Toby   Well that seems rather a coincidence.

Dr James   You're seeing what you want to see, Toby. It's what you do.

Toby   Professionally speaking, why don't you think it's the drug?

Dr James   *Professionally* speaking, two very good reasons. You asked to see the scans of the volunteers showing the greatest effect. Are you interested in who they are?

Toby   Of course.

Dr James   K. Two very different clinical histories, backgrounds, genders even. But they have one thing in common. They are both involved in an intense and protracted flirtation, with each other.

Toby   Really? Right … So you think *that's* what I'm looking at?

Dr James   I think their physical symptoms and this neural activity is a result of that … attraction and frankly it's obscuring any sense of what the drug itself is doing.

Toby   Unless it is what the drug itself is doing. If the agent is causing all these symptoms, why on earth *wouldn't* they assume they were infatuated?

Dr James   You think because they feel all the things one would associate with infatuation they are just … assuming that's what they are.

Toby   Assuming, exactly. The body responds a certain way to what it's being given, they can't sleep, they can't eat, they're in a constant state of neural excitement ever since they met, what's the brain going to conclude?

Dr James   You think it mistakes that for love?

Toby   Not even mistakes it, it creates it. To make sense of the response. Are the other volunteers showing similar effect?

Dr James   Not to the same extent.

Toby   But they're all straight men, right?

Dr James   From their hygiene levels I'd guess, yes.

Toby   Well maybe *they've* just got nowhere to go with it, nothing to hang it on. You can instil very strong feelings in a body as long as it's toward something that looks right, you know? You can make ducklings follow a kettle believing it's their mother for years.

Dr James   Can you?

Toby   They did it at Exeter.

Dr James   Oh that's very Exeter.

Toby   Looking at it objectively. With healthy volunteers we're starting from a midpoint. We're giving drugs to normal minds –

Dr James   'Normal minds.' (!)

Toby   You know what I mean. Depression's deadness of emotion, right? Insularity, lack of engagement with the world and those around you –

Dr James Is it?

Toby So the other end of the spectrum, where the agent could be taking them, is *extreme* emotion, excess engagement, overwhelming purpose and feeling. What does that sound like – ?

Dr James Bollocks?

Toby What does it sound like?

Dr James I'm pretty sure it's not drug effect, Toby (!)

Toby How? Don't forget it was just a blood pressure trial where they discovered Viagra.

Dr James So what? You're thinking you've discovered a Viagra for the heart?

Toby Don't be simplistic. It's just not impossible. Cannabis we know increases susceptibility to schizophrenia. Likewise I'm sure you can create a chemical vulnerability, to something more positive –

Dr James Sounds a bit Rohypnol to me.

Toby I mean it rather romantically! Medical science has extended everyone's lives without taking any responsibility for us having to be married longer. We could do with a bit of help!

Dr James Instead of giving up and starting over?

Mini-beat.

Toby Yeah. And you'd try anything in the worst of it.

Beat.

Dr James But we're not really talking about … attraction are we?

Toby Aren't we?

Dr James I don't think so. It seems to me you're trying to stress the chemical nature of things, for *my* benefit.

Beat.

Toby   No. But okay, yes, equally, if you have a chemical imbalance that makes you sleep all the time, feel lethargic, have trouble focusing, of course you're going to eventually feel *depressed.*

Dr James   Oh for god' s sake Toby, you ask someone about their history of depression they don't say I felt tired one day. They say, I lost my job, I lost my wife, there are external events they / respond to –

Toby   / Everybody loses their job, everybody loses their wife!

Dr James   No they don't, Toby! It's about an interaction with the world. It doesn't just appear. I know this depression as disease thing is good for business but –

Toby   Don't. Don't say that in front of me.

Dr James   Don't say that in front of *me!* I was a clinical psychiatrist at Barts for ten years while you were greasing your way up the ladder, don't tell / me what ...

Toby   / Why would you grease a ladder?!

Dr James   You know what I mean.

Toby   You weren't there a lot of those ten years.

Dr James   You don't know that at all!

Beat.

Toby   I'm sorry that's not the point.

Dr James   You don't!

Toby   And it's irrelevant.

Dr James   Are you interested in *why* I don't think it's a drug effect, Toby?

Toby   Of course, what do you *think* I'm interested in?!

Dr James   I think you're interested in whatever's most interesting.

Toby   Come on then, what makes you *so* sure this isn't our drug?

Dr James   Thank you doctor, I'm glad you asked. Because number seven here is on a placebo! All the physical symptoms *and* apparent anti-depressant effect!

Toby   Ah.

Dr James   Yes ah.

Toby   Placebo.

Dr James   Yes. So with one of them the effect's entirely natural.

A sound to indicate scan's end, resumption of trial protocol and attendance for dosing.

DOSAGE INCREASE. Text reads: Increase in dosage: 100mg

Connie *takes her dosage but goes for the wrong one.* **Dr James** *corrects her.*

Dr James   (Cont'd) No, that's not yours.

Connie   Sorry, does it matter – ?

Dr James   That one, please.

In another space **Tristan** *receives his dosage.*

Tristan   Can I go to the rec room now?

Dr James   No, you're on your own now.

Tristan   Why?

Dr James   Both of you. I'm here to monitor physiological effects, I can do without you going off creating your own.

The two lovers are kept apart. This distresses them and heightens responses.

The following in overlapped once separate spaces, as **Dr James** *records stated symptoms:*

Dr James   Anxiety? Is that what you're saying? Anxious.

Connie   Sort of. Yeah. But there's something else.

Tristan   Anxiety, yeah, but anxiety if it's good. Is there a word for that?

Connie   I do feel – yeah, I can't think of another word. But yeah.

Tristan   Alive. Really alive.

Dr James   More 'alive' than usual?

Connie   Yeah, my thoughts are racing, the speed of thought, the repetition.

Tristan   Alert, you know? Like everything's more vivid?

Connie   Can I ask you something?

Tristan   Can I ask you something?

Dr James   Sure.

Tristan   How's Connie?

Connie   Tristan. When you do these trials, someone has to *not* be on the drug right?

Tristan   Connie said the same, thoughts racing.

Dr James   What do you mean by that?

Tristan   Connie.

Connie   Tristan. Gosh, my heart.

Tristan   My heart.

Connie   Feels like it's going –

Dr James   Going – ?

Tristan   Going –

Connie   Going, you know?

Tristan   I don't know, faster.

Connie   Can you see that?

Dr James   See what?

Connie   If someone isn't on the drug, right? Sorry, I can hear my heartbeat in my ears. But you can't tell them, right?

Tristan   I just feel, vivid. Everything is vivid.

Dr James   It's not for you to worry about, much better you just tune in to what you feel.

Tristan   My mouth tastes like metal when I swallow.

Connie   Can I have some water? Sorry, oh, I'm feeling sick.

Tristan   My stomach.

Dr James   Are you going to the loo okay?

Connie   It's just a bit upset, that's all, at least I'm losing weight (!)

Tristan   I could shit through the eye of a fucking needle!

Dr James   Well we can try that later.

Connie   Oh look, God, I'm shaking.

Dr James   When did the shaking start?

Tristan   Today, right, I'm not sleeping, really, look it's stopped.

He's holding out his hand. **Connie** *is holding hers out, it's trembling.*

Connie   Is this bad?

Dr James   You're probably dehydrated.

Connie   Cos I feel –

Tristan   I feel –

Connie   I feel –

Tristan   I feel –

Connie   I feel –

Tristan   I feel like I've lost weight.

Connie   My skin looks better. But I don't know if that's, you know –

Tristan   And I don't know if this is the kind of thing you're
after –

Connie   And I don't know if this is the sort of thing you want –

Connie   (Cont'd) But I think there's an effect on um ...

Tristan   Sex drive's mental!

Connie   'Libido.'

Dr James   Right.

Tristan   I feel ... more awake.

Connie   I've never felt this alert before.

Dr James   Just try and breathe, relax, it's lights out soon. If you
can get some sleep, that would be better.

Connie   Sleep?!

Tristan   Sleep? Sleep's for the weak.

Connie   I feel like I might never sleep again (!)

Dr James   Alright. Straight back to your room now, please.
Make sure you've got your box on, yeah? Someone comes to
collect it in the morning.

Tristan *and* **Connie** *inhabit bodies racked with expectant,
alert physicality, aroused and nervy in separate rooms. They
begin texting each other on the phones that Tristan provided.
Every glowing vibrating missive is a jolt of dopamine; a high,
punctuated by a stressful low awaiting the response. They become
faster. It has the quality of shared, separate electroshock therapy
or cardiac paddles that shock. It builds, the separation fuelling it.*

Eventually **Tristan** *has snuck into her room and he watches her
comittedly typing out a message to him with affection. He receives
it silently, and, unseen, sends her another. She leaps to the phone.*

Slowly, she turns round to see him.

Connie   You shouldn't be here.

Tristan   I know.

Connie   How are you feeling?

Tristan   I feel. Full. I feel almost … holy. Like life is paying attention to me. I don't want to tell you anything about what I feel about you and what's just hit me about how I feel about you … because it's not fair when you're … I want to be good for you.

Connie   You're sweating.

Tristan   It's hot.

Connie   I'm cold.

Tristan   (*touching his sweat*) God.

Beat.

Tristan   (Cont'd) How do you feel?

Connie   Bursting. I can't stop it. Something's in me but it's like it's come from outside of me. Like having the weather inside.

Tristan   I do too.

Connie   Do you? Really?

Tristan   Yeah, I'm just not fighting it.

Connie   Tristan?

Tristan   Yeah?

Connie   Do you feel different?

Tristan   Yeah. No. I just feel … happy.

Tension. Sexual.

Tristan   (Cont'd) I'm not going to take advantage of you.

Connie   I think I'm going to take advantage of you.

Tristan   I think I'm in love.

Connie   Are you?

Tristan   Maybe you are too.

Connie   Maybe. I'm not sure what it is.

Tristan   I feel it really though.

Connie   Do you?

Tristan   If you're in love there's nothing you can do about it.

Connie   But if it's something else, something else controlling me –

Tristan   Then you're not in control.

Connie   Yes.

Tristan   Yes.

Connie   There's nothing I can do about it.

Tristan   Yes.

Beat.

Connie   I'm in love.

Tristan   Yes.

Connie   That's such a relief.

They rip off the telemetry boxes they are wearing to measure their heart rate. They make love.

Darkness.

Light. **Connie** *and* **Tristan**.

Tristan   What are you thinking?

Connie   What?

Tristan   What are you thinking?

Connie   I don't know how to begin answering that.

Tristan   Just, tell me what you're thinking.

Darkness.

Light.

Connie *is hitting* **Tristan** *with his own hand.*

Connie   What are you hitting yourself for? What are you hitting yourself for?

Tristan   I want you to hit me.

Connie   Why?

Tristan   Cos then I can show how much I don't mind.

She hits him a bit too hard and then kisses and squeals in apology.

Darkness.

Light.

Connie   I'm really heavy though.

Connie *is climbing onto* **Tristan***'s legs who is lying on his back. He balances her thighs on his feet as she balances in the air, making herself 'fly'.*

Connie   Whoo!

Tristan   Shhh!

Darkness.

Light.

Tristan   Where will we live?

Connie   Paris, New York. A farm. Anywhere.

Tristan   I'm opening a dry cleaners.

Darkness.

Light.

They look directly at each other, look away, look back.

Darkness.

Light.

Tristan   I know they don't want to see me. You know I hear that from people. But you know I would have settled. I would have – I was okay being a disappointment. I was happy to be an acceptable failure.

Darkness.

Light.

Connie *and* **Tristan** *are making love face to face.*

Connie   Ask me who's in charge.

Tristan   What?

Connie   Ask me who's in charge.

Tristan   Who's in charge?

Connie   You are.

Darkness.

In the darkness.

Connie and **Tristan**   I / I love you.

Pause Experiment Here

Wait 15 minutes.

Begin Again

A Memory:

Toby   Are you okay?

Dr James   Yeah, you?

Toby   Yeah.

Dr James   I remember with mine, it took ages. You know, years. And this nurse said to me one day, everyone dies like this now. Unless it's a motorbike crash or someone really old in their sleep, occasionally, but everyone else it's like this. A long time and really really bad.

Toby   Sure. I mean we're all supposed to be dead by now. We're designed for what, thirty or forty at most? People have kids now when they should die. (*A laugh.*)

Dr James   Sometimes I think I am. I'm dead and my body just hasn't caught up.

Toby   What?

Dr James   Don't you get that?

Toby   No (!) How's your leg?

Dr James   Oh yeah, fine.

Toby   It's more than fine, it's beautiful.

Dr James   No.

Toby   Show me the scar.

Dr James   No Toby.

They part.

Back today.

Dr James *holding a variety of tampons in her hands.* **Connie** *is choosing between them, slightly shyly.*

Dr James   (Cont'd) When did the bleeding start?

Connie   Just now. This morning.

Dr James   Before or after your dosage?

Connie   Before.

Dr James   I'm sorry I can't give you any painkillers.

Connie   I don't need any. It's just early, I think.

Dr James *pockets the surplus.*

Dr James   So. It seems your telemetry box must have come off last night while you were in bed.

Beat.

Connie   Oh, yeah, did it?

Dr James   But then you must have put it back on.

Connie   That's right.

Dr James   It's best to reattach it *before* you drift off, when you're comfortable.

Connie   (*makes to go*) Okay.

Dr James   The exact same time as Tristan's did too.

Connie   Oh.

Dr James   Looks like I'm missing eight hours of each of your hearts.

Pause. Breathing.

Dr James   (Cont'd) / Connie.

Connie   / That's weird. Sorry.

Dr James   What is it you're sorry about?

Connie   Nothing, actually. I wanted to see if he was alright, he was ill, we've both been feeling pretty dodg–

Dr James   How do you know he was feeling ill?

Connie   How do I know?

Dr James   How did you know?

Connie   Text.

Dr James   He texted you on a phone?

Connie   Yes.

Dr James   You know phones are banned, they interfere with the equipment.

Connie   I know.

Beat.

Connie   (Cont'd) How?

Dr James   Sorry?

Connie   How do they?

Dr James   The signal they give off.

Connie   What though?

Dr James   It … interferes with medical electronic devices.

Connie   It doesn't seem like that can be true though, people would just be dying everywhere wouldn't they?

Dr James   Have you had sex? I need you to be honest with me.

Beat.

Connie *(makes a sound of discomfort)*

Dr James   (Cont'd) Just answer the question, medically! Have you had sex in the last twenty-four hours?

Connie   Yes. But none of it went, where it would have to go.

Dr James   He didn't ejaculate inside you?

Connie   God (!) No! Don't write a sonnet about it.

Dr James   You know that's no protection against anything. There's still all sorts of risk.

Connie   Really? Or is that like the way phones interfere with the equipment?

Beat.

Dr James   You know you're going to have to leave.

Connie   Fine. Chuck us off. Least then I'll know.

Dr James   Not both of you. You.

Connie   Why?

Dr James   Because twinkle over there doesn't have a womb.

Connie   No! – Look, we didn't really. I'm sorry. We were just messing about. There isn't any risk of anything.

Dr James   I'm not your sex education teacher, Connie. I'm trying to run a trial, which you've put into jeopardy.

Connie   I understand there's a leasing of bodies involved here, but you can't expect to police how we feel.

Dr James   That is exactly my role. The drug is designed to stimulate transmitters that are linked to poor decision making and risk-taking –

Connie   You can't give us something that causes poor decisions and risks then have a go at us for … taking risks and making bad decisions!

Dr James   That's not a bad point but you don't know what you feel.

Connie   (*deeply distressed*) I know and it's horrible!

Dr James   This has to stop.

Connie   (*ferocious*) I think only one of us in on the drug, the way you give them out and the way I feel today I think he is and I'm not.

Dr James   During all trials someone has to be on placebo, to compare to, a control.

Connie   But if I'm on a placebo, he's on it, saying all this I can't believe him. It's driving me mad!

Dr James   That's exactly why you shouldn't be involved.

Connie   I think I might be in love with him! You have to tell me.

Dr James   I can't give you any information. It compromises the trial.

Connie   I'll just tell Tristan we both have to leave and then … then –

Beat.

Dr James   Is that what you want to do?

Beat.

Connie   At home in real life. I have a boyfriend.

Dr James   Right.

Connie   And I do love him I think. But if I did why would I – ? I keep thinking is this real, or is that ... real?

Dr James   I can't help you with that.

Connie   Why? Aren't you a psychiatrist?

Dr James   I'm a person (!)

Connie   Talk to me like a person then.

Dr James   Okay ... (?)

Beat.

Dr James   (Cont'd) I was having a rough time, quite a few years ago. I'd broken up from a long relationship I'd been in forever and that was a big decision and I'd lost a parent after a long ... time. And I was supposed to be going away for work, a conference, but I didn't know if I could, I'm afraid of flying and I nearly didn't make it. But I did, and that week turned out to be one of the best weeks of my life. Professionally and just – I met lots of interesting people and got very – you know it was good. And I got on very well with one guy there who was great and funny and a force of real joy in the room. Even though I was a mess – and well he was married – but it was one of those chance encounters that give you hope, because you think god, there are great people out there and they seem to think I'm great and ... So on the flight back I was sat next to another doctor, a woman, and she recognized me and we talked and she knew this guy and she said, oh you didn't sleep with him did you? And I say no why?! I did. So apparently he really puts it around, he's this notorious shagabout on the conference circuit and younger, less astute girls would, you know. And it was strange because it wasn't til then – ... As we flew back I sort of felt something dissolve, in the jet stream, like something got eroded down. And by the time I got back it was dark.

Connie   I'm sorry.

Dr James   No (!) I'm saying it should have ended there, that's all. But it went on.

Connie   Tristan's not like that.

Dr James   Ok.

Connie   Please. Just tell me what this is.

Beat.

Dr James   Tristan's not on the drug. Connie. He's on a placebo.

Connie   Oh.

Dr James   You see?

Connie   Right.

Dr James   So he's vulnerable in a different way.

Connie   But – he says he feels like he's on it –

Dr James   That's what happens. It's normal.

Connie   Is that okay? To lie to him like that ...?

Dr James   It's essential. You know, the history of medicine is mostly just the history of placebo since we know now almost none of it worked.

Connie   Gosh. My head. It has to stop, doesn't it.

Dr James   It has to stop. We're scheduled to increase dosage again today. If you can keep this ... you can stay.

INCREASE IN DOSAGE: 150mg

Connie *and* **Tristan** *take their pills. A moment of* **Connie** *blanking or rejecting* **Tristan**.

Tristan   Something's wrong, I can feel it.

Dr James   Wrong in what way?

Tristan   Why's Connie pissed off with me?

Dr James   I don't know that she is. I want to focus on the physical.

Tristan   I'm shaking like a leaf, I feel on the edge of a heart attack –

Dr James Really.

Tristan Yeah are you not interested?

Dr James Of course I'm interested.

Tristan Can I say anything?

Dr James You can. You're completely safe.

Tristan Quite intense thoughts. You know. Bit much.

Dr James Intrusive –

Tristan Yup. A lot of. Sexual. You know.

Dr James Okay. Well. I wonder why that might be.

Tristan Normally it's graphic, but this is … quite angry.

Dr James Right.

Tristan Do you not give a shit? Sorry (!) No actually screw it, this is your drug I'm living. I'm supposed to tell you. I feel giddy and I feel dizzy. And I feel tense.

Dr James Okay.

Tristan (*aggressively jokey*) I feel giddy. I feel giddy. (*sung*) I feel giddy and dizzy and tense!

Dr James Okay –

Tristan 'Okay'.

Dr James Is it not okay?

Tristan No, just, I tell you that and you're like. 'Okay'. Feels like, I don't know, like that joke, what's that joke, that guy in a doctor's office and he's showing him those ink blot things and he says, 'that's some people fucking' and he shows him the next one and he says, 'that's more fucking' then he shows him another one and he says, 'God that's extreme fucking fucking' And the doctor says, 'Do you ever think you might have a sexual problem?' And your man goes, 'Hey, doc, you're the one with the dirty pictures'.

Beat.

Dr James   You know humour is a great way of disguising hostility.

Beat.

He makes a noise to scare her.

Tristan   That's it not disguised, is that better? I miss Connie. I miss her mouth.

Dr James   You know she's in a relationship.

He is wounded by this and made angry.

Tristan   Yeah I know what the fuck's it to you?!

Dr James   Do you want to take a break and do this later?

Tristan   Not particularly, not fucking particularly.

Dr James   Okay.

Tristan   Why are you looking at me like that?

Dr James   I'm just noting your agitation. Is there anything else to report?

Tristan   No. Yeah. Why I was –. Look. Even if I have sexual thoughts, and I am, there's no reaction, downstairs. Nothing's happening.

Dr James   Right. Are you talking about temporary impotence?

Tristan   Well I hope it's fucking temporary. You don't want to get sued.

Dr James   For how long?

Tristan   Today and last night?

Dr James   Just today?

Tristan   That's not normal for me, okay? I know my body.

Dr James   I'm sure.

Tristan   Something's wrong.

Dr James   That must be worrying.

Tristan   Yeah.

Dr James   Are you worried something's damaged?

Tristan   But you can't look at that, can you?

Dr James   Because I'm a woman?

Tristan   No because you're not a doctor like that.

Dr James   Psychiatrists are doctors. We go to medical school and everything.

Tristan   Oh right.

Beat.

Dr James   Do you want me to –

Tristan   Are you going to have a look?

Dr James   Are you happy for me to?

Tristan   Yeah. Delighted. Fuck it. Yeah.

Dr James   Okay, do you want to just get yourself ready?

Dr James *exits, prersumably to get gloves.* **Tristan** *begins to undo/take down his trousers.*

Tristan *waits a beat, then doesn't see why he should, does up his trousers, and runs, free, to find* **Connie**. *Eventually he does. He hugs her. They kiss passionately.*

Tristan   I love you. I'm sick with missing you. (*He kisses her. She pulls away*)

Connie   No.

Tristan   What?

Connie   I want it to be fair.

Tristan   Fair? What?! Is this about him? Have you talked to him?

Connie   I'm just trying to keep this safe.

Tristan   Safe? Are you frightened of me now?

Connie   No. Should I be?

Tristan   Yeah I'm a fucking monster. Just say what you mean.

Connie   I am. I'm saying no.

Tristan   To what?

Connie   I'm in a relationship and you're clearly not a relationship kind of guy –

Tristan   Where did that come from?!

Connie   You're a flirty, you know, bit of a player type –

Tristan   No I'm not!

Connie   I've seen you flirt with the doctor for god's sake.

Tristan   Are you joking? Christ Connie, she's nearly fifty!

Connie   Yeah, are you saying women can't be attractive in their forties?!

Tristan   What, I'm the one that's been flirting with her apparently! … Has she been saying things about me?

Connie   It's none of your business.

Tristan   You're not telling me something.

Connie   You're being weird.

Tristan   You're lying.

Connie   I haven't said anything, how can I be lying?!

Tristan   By not telling me stuff.

Connie   There's loads of stuff I'm not telling you all the time, otherwise it would be unbearable!

Tristan   That's exactly the sort of thing people say when they're lying.

She runs her hands through her hair in stress. Her hair comes out in her hands.

Connie   My hair's coming out.

Tristan   Mine's coming out too.

Connie   Yeah but not because of the drug.

Tristan   Fuck you.

Connie   I didn't mean that!

Tristan   Just don't rewrite what's happened. Don't make out /
I'm –

Connie   / I'm not! What do you care anyway? That's in the past.
I thought you wanted to live *now?*

Tristan   I want *you* to live *now.* You're always talking about
what happens afterwards or how we got here, tell me what you
feel *now?*

Connie   It doesn't matter what I feel, what does it matter –

Tristan   / Because I'm asking you!

Connie   I don't know!

Tristan   You're so scared. Why are you so scared all the time?!
It's like being with an old woman. What might go wrong though?

Connie   This is my life!

Tristan   Exactly!

Connie   You don't care do you?

Tristan   Course I do.

Connie   Because you just want it NOW. You know maybe you
should start thinking about the future a bit.

Tristan   What?!

Connie   This isn't exactly a gap year, Tris. It's become a sort of
gap life.

Tristan   That's a terrible thing to say to me.

Connie   Then don't say I'm boring just cos I'm not giving you what you want!

Tristan   Are you saying I'm not good enough for you?

Connie   No I'm saying sort your*self* out / –

Tristan   / I'm punching above my weight?

Connie   – before you make out I'm a coward. I'm happy with my life.

Tristan   Ha! Yeah course you are, you look happy, you look fucking delighted!

Connie   You've got no idea how I feel.

Tristan   TELL ME!

Connie   You're like a child.

Tristan   I'm fine for a quick fuck but secretly you want the older, duller man who's gonna *provide* and bring some cash to the fucking table?

Connie   Oh my god /

Tristan   That's basically what you said –

Connie   / what are we even talking about?!

Tristan   Gap Life!

Connie   I'm the one that's sat there and watched you do your cheeky twinkly stuff with the doctor and you were a bit of a sleaze with me early on what am I supposed to think?!

Tristan   I don't – You're the one in a relationship, as you keep going on / about

Connie   *You* go on about it!

Tristan   – I'm allowed! I can do what I like!

Connie   Oh so I'm a slag now?

Tristan   No! Put away your paranoia, love.

Connie   Don't call me love. It's so tacky.

Beat.

Tristan   Connie. Con. Come on. Kiss and make up.

Connie   No, I feel sick.

Tristan   I make you sick (?)

Connie   I didn't say that. I'm not going to kiss you. I don't want to be sick on you.

Tristan   I don't care. Be sick in my mouth. I'll eat it up.

Connie   I *said* I feel sick!

Tristan   Am I a bit coarse for you? Is that it? Are you used to something more refined? Some wine drinking chino wearing cunt?

Connie   You don't get to talk about him, you understand?

Tristan   I wasn't! Is that what he's like! Came to mind pretty fast!

Connie   You keep shaking up my view of him and I think it's manipulative –

Tristan   Of course it's fucking manipulative!

Connie   You've never met him!

Tristan   That's why it's easy to slag him off! Come on, it's a joke!

Connie   It's a joke. Your way of getting out of everything. It's a joke. So now I'm a slag with no sense of humour.

Tristan   Oh my god, you're insane.

Connie   Everything I'm saying makes sense if there's a problem it's with you understanding!

She makes a gesture of his stupidity. He frustratedly roars at her.

Connie   (Cont'd) What do you *want* to happen? I mean, really?

Tristan   I'll tell you what I want. I don't want to *reason* with you. I want to know right now, in this moment, what you *feel*.

Beat.

Connie   I ... I feel. Oh god. I think I don't love you the way that you love me.

Ow. (Pause.)

Tristan   Right. Well you want me to look into the future. Fine. Go home. Suck on his old cock. Stay with him for two years longer than you should, out of guilt for him having left his wife and kid for you –

Connie   He didn't –

Tristan   Tell yourself you've invested so much now and it was nothing with me and you're getting rougher looking while he's staying the same and he's a good dad and before you know it you're forty-five, fucked and caring for some old cunt with cancer.

Connie *bends double with the pain of it.*

Connie   I hate you.

Tristan   Have you been calling / him?

Connie   / I physically hate you.

Tristan   – telling him everything's fine, you miss him. Have you used my fucking phone to do that?!

Connie   You gave it to me.

Tristan   Give it to me.

Connie   I don't have it.

Tristan   You're a liar.

Connie   You're scaring me.

During, there's a tussle. He gets the phone and practisedly looks through it. He throws it on the floor and smashes it.

Beat.

Connie (Cont'd) (*cold*) You just broke your own phone you stupid Irish cunt.

They physically fight. She ends up getting hurt and this becomes clear.

Connie (Cont'd) Stop. Tris.

He sees she is bleeding. She sees she is bleeding. To him it is a tragedy, to her it is a triumph. He backs away, in distress. Then to her, in sorrow.

Tristan I'm sorry. Sorry. It's the drugs.

Connie *Now* it is?!

Tristan (*crying*) I can't handle it.

Connie Stop it.

Tristan I'm losing it.

Connie Bullshit. You're not even on the / drug, Tristan.

Tristan / I'm having a whitey.

He seems about to be sick.

Connie You're not on it. She told me.

Tristan What?

Connie You're on a placebo. This is all just you.

His body tries to absorb the information.

A man in a doorway. His shoulders heave with breathing. It's **Toby**.

Dr James I feel like something awful's going to happen.

Toby … Okay.

Dr James I think we should exclude one of the volunteers from the trial. A boy, a guy, the man who's on placebo in fact. He's not dealing with the environment. He's shown aggression and instability, now he's not eating. In any other environment I'd be worried for his mental health.

Toby   They've been in a sealed ward for weeks now, anyone would get frustrated –

Dr James   It may be linked to his relationship with the other volunteer.

Toby   There's only one dosage left, surely invalidating the trial –

Dr James   It's not going to invalidate the trial, removing one control subject –

Toby   We have a duty of care to him at this stage.

Dr James   No we don't, he's clean! We can just discharge him today – !

Toby   That's not appropriate.

Dr James   I'm used to helping people, you know, not putting them in a situation that distresses them. I don't think I can do this.

Toby   Yes you can.

Dr James   Is it me? I'm terrified it's me. Have I done something? It doesn't make any sense.

Toby   Okay, Lorna … Calm down. This isn't what you think. He is a test subject. His symptoms are relevant. And we need to monitor him as such.

Dr James   I give out the pills, Toby, /

Toby   / You don't know what you're giving out. They're active agent just packaged differently. Deliberately. He's on the drug. We're testing practitioner bias, alongside. As well. To see if there's a difference in what you report, according to what you think they're being given.

Dr James   You're testing *me*?!

Toby   It's not un/ usual –

Dr James   You're testing *me!*

Toby   I know how you feel about all this and I *still* got you the position here, because I know you're a good / doctor.

Dr James   / Oh god okay, I'm grateful. Thank you Mr Raushen, thank you for picking me up off the street in your limo on the way to the next expo –

Toby   All we're doing is monitoring you for practitioner bias which we often do with new recruits –

Dr James   Bullshit

Toby   – In key areas, and I know you're feeling exposed –

Dr James   You lied

Toby   – or confused and you know that's an irrational response.

Dr James   I thought I was losing it! That's why you're testing me isn't it? So our volunteer *is* being medicated with powerful psychiatric drugs and I'm telling you they cause aggressive behaviour and paranoia, it's dangerous to continue.

Toby   We don't know that's the drug! You just said, you said yourself it's about the relationship with this girl! I'm not closing down a whole trial because of a lovers' tiff!

Dr James   (This can't be pulled apart. We're crazy to think it can.)

Toby   This is why we do trials! We're here to record side effects and if aggression is a side effect, we'll note it.

Dr James   There's no such thing as side effects, Toby, they're just effects *you* can't sell.

Toby   God that's bitter, Lorna.

Dr James   I've seen you hold that brain and fleece them for money. But somehow *I'm* the one that's biased – (!)

Toby   You sound it, listen to yourself. You've spent this whole time refusing to accept the drugs have any effect, until you think there's something damaging!

Dr James   You literally only publish trials with the results you like!? But apparently you're unbiased and I'm … What?

Toby   You are a good doctor, who suffers from profound depressive episodes which she refuses to medicate. And you're desperate for any evidence that supports that position.

Beat.

Dr James   (They don't work)

Toby   Pardon?

Dr James   They don't.

Toby   How would you know?

Dr James   There's no real evidence for the efficacy of anti-depressants, there never has been. / Everyone who knows, knows this has been the biggest disaster in the history of medicine!

Toby   (*in frustration*) / Mmmmmmmm. you can do what you like but you can't speak for most people. Most people improve on anti-depressants.

Dr James   In the short term!

Toby   If you're going to kill yourself tomorrow, what do you care if it's short term? Every time you have an episode, every time, the brain is altered and makes the next one longer and deeper. The sooner you start to medicate, the more you protect yourself. You could have done that –

Dr James   What, forever?

Toby   No! Or yes, depending how you are, it's very common –

Dr James   It's not an it, Toby, we're talking about me! What if it's a symptom, not a disease? What if it's a useful pain, throbbing, saying 'change your life, change your life' then you come with your pills and take all that away –

Toby   Well you never took them, Lorn, how'd your life go?

Dr James   Fuck you! You know us so called depressed people actually have a more accurate view of the world, a more realistic view of ourselves and others –

Toby   In mild and moderate depression, yes.

Dr James   Who are the vast majority being medicated! We're not deluded, you are.

Toby   This is why I get annoyed, Lorna. You cling to the mystery. You celebrate it, almost.

Dr James   I do what?!

Toby   You don't want it to be curable, you want to make it grand and tragic, it doesn't have to be.

Dr James   You think I *like* it! You think I like it!?

Toby   It doesn't make it less to accept it's chemical. It *helps* most people.

Dr James. Say I'm mad if you like. But don't say I've got a disease.

Toby   Call it what you like, –

Dr James   Oh thank you –

Toby   All I've ever wanted is to help you.

Dr James   I don't want your help!

Toby   I know and it's infuriating!

Beat.

Dr James   I swear, Toby, we're going to look back at this chemical imbalance shit like it's the four humours all over again. I mean, why am I here?

Toby   What, *here?*

Dr James   Yes. Why would you offer me work? This isn't what I do. I sit with people, I talk to them, I –

Toby   I want to help.

Dr James   Yeah but why? You see, I wonder if you feel guilty.

Toby   About you?

Dr James   Yes.

Toby   Not particularly.

Dr James   Not particularly?

Toby   Is this what we should be talking about now?

Dr James   I don't know. What do you think?

Toby   Are you saying you think I caused it?

Dr James *is silent. A therapist's silence.*

Toby   I don't think I caused it, Lorna.

Dr James   Then why am I here?

Toby   You're a good doctor.

Dr James   Then why are you testing me?

Beat.

Toby   I didn't cause it and it's a cruel thing to say.

Dr James   I didn't say it. You did. You seem upset.

Toby   Just –

Dr James   It was years ago.

Toby   I know.

Dr James   And I've had what you'd call episodes since then.

Toby   I know.

Dr James   So why do you feel so bad? Look at me. It's not your fault, Toby. In the mountain of shit the world dumped on me that year, the dump you took was minor. It was barely a contributor. It could have been anything or anyone. So don't *you* make it into some big thing.

Beat.

Toby   I don't think I caused your depression, by ending things, Lorna. I don't think I contributed even. But maybe, maybe I think I ended it *because* of your depression.

Dr James   Right.

Toby   And maybe that's worse.

Dr James   No. Just sad. And are you happy now?

Toby   Well not right now, but yes.

Dr James   So. And how old is she, this new one?

Toby   What does that have to do with anything?

Dr James   Just wondering. Twenty-eight? Twenty-nine? You're so keen to make me a prisoner of my insides. What about you? Her clear skin to indicate lack of disease? Waist not yet travelled up to her tits? All the signs of the fertility that you don't actually want? We're all just walking examples of a biological fact, Toby.

Toby   You're ill, Lorn. Please.

Dr James   I'm not though.

Toby   My choices, or biology, or whatever, don't cause me suffering.

Dr James   No, only others. So you'll be fine. You'll do fine. (*Pause.*)

Toby   It's entirely within our rights to assess you. It was never an indication of any lack of faith. I want you to finish this trial. I think you can do it. Then we'll talk about the future.

Dr James   (Fine.)

Dr James *leaves.*

Connie   Tris … Tris?

Connie   I love you. You can feel that (?)

Tristan   I don't know what that is.

Connie   (*desperate*) Yes you do! You do.

Tristan   (*untouched*) This is horrible.

Connie   I can't bear it when you're sad in case I caused it. And I can't bear it when you're happy in case I didn't.

Tristan   Sometimes I think I'll only be happy when you're dead.

They look at each other, and away, appalled.

Dr James *enters and begins preparing doses.*

Text Reads:

Final dosage, highest toleration: 250mg single dose

Toby *enters and observes.* **Dr James** *facilitates, resenting* **Toby**'s *stare and the drugs themselves.*

The final dosages are administered with the usual countdowns **Tristan** *first.*

Dr James   5, 4, 3, 2, 1

Tristan *tosses his dose back with contempt for its nothingness.*

Dr James   (Cont'd) 5, 4, 3, 2, 1.

Connie, *anxious, gets given hers.* **Dr James** *avoids checking her mouth afterwards as she is glaring at* **Toby**. *In the moment,* **Connie** *rushes to* **Tristan** *and kisses him full on the mouth. She's kept her pill in to transfer to him, which the kiss does. She covers his mouth with her hand to encourage him to swallow.*

Connie   (I love you.)

He makes the decision to swallow her pill. They look into each other's eyes. **Dr James** *notices something.*

Dr James   What's going on, / what did you do?

Toby   / What's happened?

Dr James   (*to* **Tristan**) Show me the inside of your mouth.

She checks the inside if his mouth with a light, then his eyes as she sees his pupils are dilating.

Dr James   (Cont'd) Is everything okay, Tris/tan?

Toby   / Did he take something else?

Toby *seeks to intervene,* **Dr James** *turns to* **Connie** *who is worried they are going to stop him swallowing. This all happens quickly.*

Connie   No, let him!

Dr James   Did you give / him something else?

Toby   / Is your name Tristan? I'm Toby. Have you taken anything else?

Tristan   I'm / fine.

Dr James   / How much have you given him?

Tristan   Connie?

Connie   I'm here.

Tristan   You've got a … halo …

Dr James   Tristan?

Tristan *makes a strange sound, he staggers, loses consciousness, falls to the floor, stiffens. His limbs jerk and twitch. His mouth gurns. He is fitting. He bleeds from his mouth and wets himself. It is horrific.*

A scuffle.

Connie *withdraws at the close up and puts her hands over her ears briefly in shock then begins tearing at her skin.*

Connie   Get it out get it out of me!

An alarm and darkness.

Connie *is taken away.*

Dr James *is left to clean up.*

Dr James *has a bucket in which she finds a brain.*

Dr James   All we are is this three pound lump of jelly. But it's not necessarily me is it? I want to be happy. I want to work hard.

I want to not shout out swear words on the street. I want to sleep. It must know this. It must want that too. If it's me. But. Here I am, where my father held me on a climbing frame and I can see my shoes on the bar. Here, how much I like meringue. Here's my respiration control. Here's my impulse to kill myself. Here is my controlling that impulse. 'You're disgusting. And you're only going to get more disgusting. It's too late. This all gets worse and you can't even cope with now'. Shhh. Let's not. 'You're like your mother'. It's too hard. Other people manage (!) And still. 'You can't do anything. You can't work, well you could but you're lazy. This is the best you're capable of looking now and it's shit and you're decaying. Look at your teeth. And everything everyone says about you is right. And you're weak and you're a coward and you've ruined people's lives. And you should have done it a long time ago and you never will now'. Just put some clothes on and then we'll go from there.,It would be better'. Just put on some pants. Then we'll deal with the next bit. Just do that. 'It would be better just to stop'. But people love you.,No they don't. Even the people who love you hate you because you're hurting the person they love. Why can't you stop?

Collapse.

Eventually ...

Now it is **Tristan** *in a bed on a drip.*

Connie *enters, looks at him. Eventually, he sees her.*

Tristan   I'm thirsty. Do you have water?

She sees there is water, or gets water from her bag.

Connie   Hello.

Tristan   What day is it? You look scared. What happened? Is it me? What happened? (*He touches his face.*)

Connie   It's Friday.

Tristan   I don't know anyone. Why am I here? You look frightened? What happened?

Connie   You've had a blood transfusion. They told me you have something called transient global amnesia.

Tristan   Yes. Have I? Yes. Why are you looking at me, am I still me?

Connie   Yeah. You just have new blood. It's okay. (*He panics.*)

Tristan   Can I see?

Connie   See what?

Tristan   I need a mirror.

Connie   Oh.

She thinks, looks round, scrabbles in bag, opens up a bit of make up with a tiny one, hands it over.

Tristan *stares at bits of his face, waving it around to get sections of face and so a fuller picture. She stares at him.*

Tristan   What's happening? What day is it?

Connie   It's Friday. It's your birthday.

Tristan   How is that today? Show me a thing saying that's today.

Connie   The date?

Tristan   Yeah.

She hunts, comes up with only her phone and shows it to him.

Tristan   (Cont'd) You could have changed that.

Connie   Why would I do that?

Tristan   Have I been asleep then?

Connie   You've got something called transient global amnesia.

Tristan   Yes, I – transient, does that mean –

Connie   It's going to pass. They don't know when or how long –

Tristan   What was I doing before you got here?

Connie   I don't know. I wasn't here.

Tristan   What day is it?

Connie   Friday. It's your birthday.

Tristan   No. Is it? Something else.

Connie   That it's my birthday too. You remember that?

Tristan   No. Oh god oh god oh god.

Connie   You don't know me, do you? You're not retaining any new memories it's me, you know me, do you know my name?

He does not reply.

Connie   How do you feel?

Tristan   I'm hungry.

Connie *finds a yoghurt and gives it to him.*

Connie   We were on a trial. Do you remember?

Tristan   I'm not being stupid, something awful's happened, I don't know where I am!

Connie   You're in the hospital. Do you know what day it is?

Tristan   Yes.

Connie   It's okay if you don't.

Tristan   What day is it?

Connie   Friday.

Tristan *looks at the yoghurt in his hand. Meaning drains from it. He offers it to* **Connie**.

Tristan   Is this yours?

Connie   I'm going to feed you this yoghurt right now.

Tristan   Okay.

Connie   And then we'll go from there.

A glimpse of **Dr James** *who has taken to bed with depression.*

Connie *enters, casual, busy.* **Tristan** *is in bed. He is alert but blank.*

Tristan   I don't know anybody here. Why am I here?

Connie   Shh, it's okay. I know. I was just here.

Tristan   No, you don't understand, I just woke up!

Connie   I know, you've got something called transient global amnesia –

Tristan   Transient, does that mean –

Connie   Yes it's going to pass.

Tristan   What day is it?

Connie   It's Tuesday.

Tristan   Is that right?! Show me something, with the date on.

Connie *gives him a newspaper, practisedly. She gets out a mirror, practisedly, he looks at himself.*

Tristan   (Cont'd) I have to go! I – why am I here?

Connie   You're having trouble remembering, forming new memories.

Tristan   I'm trying to think the last thing I remember.

Connie   That's okay.

Tristan   But I know you.

Connie   That's right, Tris.

She begins giving him a bed bath.

Connie   (Cont'd) That's right. Before the seizure. You and me were on a trial. Weeks ago.

Tristan   Do you work here?

Connie   No. That's new, do I work here (!) How do you feel?

Tristan   Awful. My balls ache.

Connie   I bet they do. You've got a stiffy all the time. God knows why.

Tristan   I'm scared.

Connie   I know.

Tristan   I'm hot.

Connie   I know.

Tristan   I feel sick.

Connie   Relax.

She looks around. She touches his erection under the sheets.

Connie   Always. Poor thing.

Tristan   Jesus.

She masturbates him.

(*He sighs, relaxes.*)

Tristan   (Cont'd) I thought you were my sister, maybe. – You're not, are you? Actually no don't tell me.

Connie   No. I do this most days. I love how you're funny. I would have thought you needed memory to be funny.

Tristan   I thought you were here to give me a bath.

Connie   Well do you want this or do you want the bath, cos there's no point giving you the bath first.

Tristan   No. This.

She masturbates him. It's affectionate but practical. When he's ejaculated she finishes washing him, and her hand. She pecks him on the cheek.

Tristan   (Cont'd) Am I your boyfriend?

Connie   I broke up with my boyfriend.

Tristan   I'm sorry. I'm trying to remember the last thing I remember. What day is it?

Connie   It's Sunday. Do you remember me, Tris?

Tristan   You're who I know.

Connie   Yes but who is that?

Tristan   I – wait –

Connie   How many times d'you think we've had this conversation?

Tristan   You don't understand I can't remember waking up! I wasn't there! Oh god this is terrible! Get someone, for god's sake!

Connie   We say this every day.

Tristan   No!

Tristan   What day is it?

Connie   It's Wednesday. How do you feel? Are you thirsty?

Tristan   I'm freaked out. I'm trying to think what the last thing I was doing was.

Connie   I had a haircut.

Tristan   I can't remember anything.

Connie   I know. I'm sorry I was joking.

Tristan   What's going on?

Tristan   Something's really wrong I can't, there's nothing going on before this?!

Connie   I know.

Tristan   What – ?

Connie   It's Tuesday.

Tristan   What – ?

Connie   You had a bad reaction on a trial.

Tristan   Where?

Connie   Hospital. You have a thing.

Tristan   –?

Connie   Here.

She gives him a mirror.

Connie   (Cont'd) Here.

She gives him a paper. She gets out a nail file.

He looks baffled.

Connie   (Cont'd) This is the day we do your nails.

She files his nails.

Tristan   Do I love you ...?

Beat. This is new.

Connie   I don't know. Do you?

Tristan   I don't know.

Beat. She absorbs this.

Connie   If you're there. Help me. I don't care what it was I see that now. You were right. I just want one conversation like it used to be so you can help me. You won't believe this but I swear, I would rather get old and argue with you every day than ever love anyone else.

Tristan   Why are you sad?

Dr James *in a bed.*

Toby *enters. He has a cup with pills in it.*

Dr James *can't really respond properly socially eye contact and natural limbic response is all gone. Its like she's elderly and exhausted. All social response and interaction takes effort, which she does her best to provide, and they are received with a grateful understanding for that.*

Toby   Hey you. Still here I see. Thought you might have made a break for it.

Toby   (Cont'd) It's crazy weather today. Can't decide anything.

Toby   (Cont'd) They wanted me to bang on at you about the fluoxetine again but I know you hate it and it's not my favourite either to be honest.

Toby   (Cont'd) Do you want to know about anything else?

Dr James   (What about the boy?)

Toby   Well obviously we don't know what the long-term effects will be yet. Turns out he had history of childhood seizures which was undisclosed so that's … Nothing will be published obviously.

She indicates she wants to know about **Toby**.

Dr James   (What about you?)

Toby   Oh I'm okay. Don't worry. The lecture circuit. Lining up round the – . And I think now I might finally write that book.

Dr James   I'm sorry.

Toby   Don't be sorry.

She doesn't accept this.

Beat.

Toby   (Cont'd) Wait, I can tell you something about the boy, he's going home with her, the girl from the trial. He's in recovery but …

It still hurts her and she blames herself.

Toby   (Cont'd) It's not your fault.

Dr James   I don't have enough skin.

She cries.

Dr James   (Cont'd) I just want to go. I want to go.

Toby   No no no.

Dr James   I'm sorry.

Toby   This is a storm. It passes.

She doesn't believe this.

Toby   (Cont'd) I love you, Lorn. And it's not romantic with …
the lies of that, and it's not family, like, a genetic trick. I just. I've
built a bit of my brain round you. And it's important to me. So.
Please.

This is too much emotion.

Toby   (Cont'd) Do you want me to go?

She's emotionally exhausted. She nods.

Toby   (Cont'd) I'm coming back tomorrow. I am. I've got a thing
in the morning but I'll do my best. Please will you think about
things for me?

He leaves a cup with drugs in for her.

Around her, but in a different space, **Connie** *and* **Tristan** *have
been getting his things together to leave his ward. He is okay,
but vulnerable, his physicality is of a different man, without some
former bounce. She is practical, tired, supportive.*

Connie   What else?

Tristan   That's the lot.

Connie   Your shoelace.

Tristan   It's alright. I don't have any change.

Connie   It's okay, I got a cab. I told you.

Tristan   A cab (!) I'd have got the bus.

Connie   I know you would. I want a cab. We'll get cash out on
the way. Did I do the drawer?

He looks. He's not sure. She checks.

Connie   (Cont'd) I'm really nervous about you seeing it. It's a
shithole.

Tristan   What is?

Connie   Where we're going back to. Mine.

Tristan   Why?

Connie   Because that's what we're doing today.

They head towards the door.

Connie   (Cont'd) Why don't you just do it up?

Tristan   What? It doesn't matter.

She bends down to do his shoelace up. He doesn't want this and goes to do it himself.

Tristan   (Cont'd) Fine.

He does bend down and does the laces.

Tristan   (Cont'd) I'm not doing it up cos I can't. I honestly couldn't be arsed.

Connie   (*during*) (That's worse)

Tristan   (*joking*) Oh, will you … (shut up woman)

It takes him longer to do than it should an adult, but eventually he does.

He finishes.

Tristan   (Cont'd) Is it cold?

Connie   It's coldish.

He adjusts some clothing appropriately. They both look around the room.

Connie   (Cont'd) Right. Okay? Oh.

She suddenly checks her bag/pockets, looks round the room.

Tristan   Y'alright?

Connie   Yeah just thought I'd lost my phone. No there it is. Okay. Happy?

Tristan   Yeah. You?

Connie   Yeah.

Tristan   Okay.

Connie   Let's go.

Connie *and* **Tristan**, *unsmiling, together, walk out into the real world.*

Dr James, *alone, looks at the cup/pills Toby left, decides, and after counting down from five in her head, takes them.*

Underneath this we hear the sound of an EEG: Electrical activity in the brain produced by neurons firing. Underpinning this is the bass of a heart beat from an ECG. These are the sounds of human love.

End experiment.